KOREAN
VOCABULARY

ENGLISH-
KOREAN

The most useful words
To expand your lexicon and sharpen
your language skills

5000 words

Korean vocabulary for English speakers - 5000 words
By Andrey Taranov

T&P Books vocabularies are intended for helping you learn, memorize and review foreign words. The dictionary is divided into themes, covering all major spheres of everyday activities, business, science, culture, etc.

The process of learning words using T&P Books' theme-based dictionaries gives you the following advantages:

- Correctly grouped source information predetermines success at subsequent stages of word memorization
- Availability of words derived from the same root allowing memorization of word units (rather than separate words)
- Small units of words facilitate the process of establishing associative links needed for consolidation of vocabulary
- Level of language knowledge can be estimated by the number of learned words

T&P Books Publishing
www.tpbooks.com

ISBN: 978-1-78616-607-4

This book is also available in E-book formats.
Please visit www.tpbooks.com or the major online bookstores.

KOREAN VOCABULARY
for English speakers

T&P Books vocabularies are intended to help you learn, memorize, and review foreign words. The vocabulary contains over 5000 commonly used words arranged thematically.

- Vocabulary contains the most commonly used words
- Recommended as an addition to any language course
- Meets the needs of beginners and advanced learners of foreign languages
- Convenient for daily use, revision sessions, and self-testing activities
- Allows you to assess your vocabulary

Special features of the vocabulary

- Words are organized according to their meaning, not alphabetically
- Words are presented in three columns to facilitate the reviewing and self-testing processes
- Words in groups are divided into small blocks to facilitate the learning process
- The vocabulary offers a convenient and simple transcription of each foreign word

The vocabulary has 155 topics including:

Basic Concepts, Numbers, Colors, Months, Seasons, Units of Measurement, Clothing & Accessories, Food & Nutrition, Restaurant, Family Members, Relatives, Character, Feelings, Emotions, Diseases, City, Town, Sightseeing, Shopping, Money, House, Home, Office, Working in the Office, Import & Export, Marketing, Job Search, Sports, Education, Computer, Internet, Tools, Nature, Countries, Nationalities and more ...

T&P BOOKS' THEME-BASED DICTIONARIES

The Correct System for Memorizing Foreign Words

Acquiring vocabulary is one of the most important elements of learning a foreign language, because words allow us to express our thoughts, ask questions, and provide answers. An inadequate vocabulary can impede communication with a foreigner and make it difficult to understand a book or movie well.

The pace of activity in all spheres of modern life, including the learning of modern languages, has increased. Today, we need to memorize large amounts of information (grammar rules, foreign words, etc.) within a short period. However, this does not need to be difficult. All you need to do is to choose the right training materials, learn a few special techniques, and develop your individual training system.

Having a system is critical to the process of language learning. Many people fail to succeed in this regard; they cannot master a foreign language because they fail to follow a system comprised of selecting materials, organizing lessons, arranging new words to be learned, and so on. The lack of a system causes confusion and eventually, lowers self-confidence.

T&P Books' theme-based dictionaries can be included in the list of elements needed for creating an effective system for learning foreign words. These dictionaries were specially developed for learning purposes and are meant to help students effectively memorize words and expand their vocabulary.

Generally speaking, the process of learning words consists of three main elements:

- Reception (creation or acquisition) of a training material, such as a word list
- Work aimed at memorizing new words
- Work aimed at reviewing the learned words, such as self-testing

All three elements are equally important since they determine the quality of work and the final result. All three processes require certain skills and a well-thought-out approach.

New words are often encountered quite randomly when learning a foreign language and it may be difficult to include them all in a unified list. As a result, these words remain written on scraps of paper, in book margins, textbooks, and so on. In order to systematize such words, we have to create and continually update a "book of new words." A paper notebook, a netbook, or a tablet PC can be used for these purposes.

This "book of new words" will be your personal, unique list of words. However, it will only contain the words that you came across during the learning process. For example, you might have written down the words "Sunday," "Tuesday," and "Friday." However, there are additional words for days of the week, for example, "Saturday," that are missing, and your list of words would be incomplete. Using a theme dictionary, in addition to the "book of new words," is a reasonable solution to this problem.

The theme-based dictionary may serve as the basis for expanding your vocabulary.

It will be your big "book of new words" containing the most frequently used words of a foreign language already included. There are quite a few theme-based dictionaries available, and you should ensure that you make the right choice in order to get the maximum benefit from your purchase.

Therefore, we suggest using theme-based dictionaries from T&P Books Publishing as an aid to learning foreign words. Our books are specially developed for effective use in the sphere of vocabulary systematization, expansion and review.

Theme-based dictionaries are not a magical solution to learning new words. However, they can serve as your main database to aid foreign-language acquisition. Apart from theme dictionaries, you can have copybooks for writing down new words, flash cards, glossaries for various texts, as well as other resources; however, a good theme dictionary will always remain your primary collection of words.

T&P Books' theme-based dictionaries are specialty books that contain the most frequently used words in a language.

The main characteristic of such dictionaries is the division of words into themes. For example, the *City* theme contains the words "street," "crossroads," "square," "fountain," and so on. The *Talking* theme might contain words like "to talk," "to ask," "question," and "answer".

All the words in a theme are divided into smaller units, each comprising 3–5 words. Such an arrangement improves the perception of words and makes the learning process less tiresome. Each unit contains a selection of words with similar meanings or identical roots. This allows you to learn words in small groups and establish other associative links that have a positive effect on memorization.

The words on each page are placed in three columns: a word in your native language, its translation, and its transcription. Such positioning allows for the use of techniques for effective memorization. After closing the translation column, you can flip through and review foreign words, and vice versa. "This is an easy and convenient method of review – one that we recommend you do often."

Our theme-based dictionaries contain transcriptions for all the foreign words. Unfortunately, none of the existing transcriptions are able to convey the exact nuances of foreign pronunciation. That is why we recommend using the transcriptions only as a supplementary learning aid. Correct pronunciation can only be acquired with the help of sound. Therefore our collection includes audio theme-based dictionaries.

The process of learning words using T&P Books' theme-based dictionaries gives you the following advantages:

- You have correctly grouped source information, which predetermines your success at subsequent stages of word memorization
- Availability of words derived from the same root (lazy, lazily, lazybones), allowing you to memorize word units instead of separate words
- Small units of words facilitate the process of establishing associative links needed for consolidation of vocabulary
- You can estimate the number of learned words and hence your level of language knowledge
- The dictionary allows for the creation of an effective and high-quality revision process
- You can revise certain themes several times, modifying the revision methods and techniques
- Audio versions of the dictionaries help you to work out the pronunciation of words and develop your skills of auditory word perception

The T&P Books' theme-based dictionaries are offered in several variants differing in the number of words: 1.500, 3.000, 5.000, 7.000, and 9.000 words. There are also dictionaries containing 15,000 words for some language combinations. Your choice of dictionary will depend on your knowledge level and goals.

We sincerely believe that our dictionaries will become your trusty assistant in learning foreign languages and will allow you to easily acquire the necessary vocabulary.

TABLE OF CONTENTS

PRONUNCIATION GUIDE

Letter	Korean example	T&P phonetic alphabet	English example

Consonants

Letter	Korean example	T&P phonetic alphabet	English example
ㄱ [1]	개	[k]	clock, kiss
ㄱ [2]	아기	[g]	game, gold
ㄲ	껌	[k]	tense [k]
ㄴ	눈	[n]	name, normal
ㄷ [3]	달	[t]	tourist, trip
ㄷ [4]	사다리	[d]	day, doctor
ㄸ	딸	[t]	tense [t]
ㄹ [5]	라디오	[r]	rice, radio
ㄹ [6]	십팔	[l]	lace, people
ㅁ	문	[m]	magic, milk
ㅂ [7]	봄	[p]	pencil, private
ㅂ [8]	아버지	[b]	baby, book
ㅃ	빵	[p]	tense [p]
ㅅ [9]	실	[s]	city, boss
ㅅ [10]	옷	[t]	tourist, trip
ㅆ	쌀	[ja:]	royal
ㅇ [11]	강	[ŋg]	language, single
ㅈ [12]	집	[tɕ]	cheer
ㅈ [13]	아주	[dʑ]	jeans, gene
ㅉ	짬	[tɕ]	tense [tch]
ㅊ	차	[tɕh]	hitchhiker
ㅌ	택시	[th]	don't have
ㅋ	칼	[kh]	work hard
ㅍ	포도	[ph]	top hat
ㅎ	한국	[h]	home, have

Letter	Korean example	T&P phonetic alphabet	English example

Vowels and combinations with vowels

ㅏ	사	[a]	shorter than in ask
ㅑ	향	[ja]	Kenya, piano
ㅓ	머리	[ʌ]	lucky, sun
ㅕ	병	[jɑ]	young, yard
ㅗ	몸	[o]	pod, John
ㅛ	표	[jɔ]	New York
ㅜ	물	[u]	book
ㅠ	슈퍼	[ju]	youth, usually
ㅡ	음악	[ɪ]	big, America
ㅣ	길	[i], [i:]	feet, Peter
ㅐ	뱀	[ɛ], [ɛ:]	habit, bad
ㅒ	애기	[je]	yesterday, yen
ㅔ	펜	[e]	elm, medal
ㅖ	계산	[je]	yesterday, yen
ㅘ	왕	[wa]	watt, white
ㅙ	왜	[ʋə]	pure, fuel
ㅚ	회의	[ø], [we]	first, web
ㅝ	권	[uɔ]	to order, to open
ㅞ	웬	[ʋə]	pure, fuel
ㅟ	쥐	[wi]	whiskey
ㅢ	거의	[ɯi]	combination [ɪi]

Comments

[1]   at the beginning of words
[2]   between voiced sounds
[3]   at the beginning of words
[4]   between voiced sounds
[5]   at the beginning of a syllable
[6]   at the end of a syllable
[7]   at the beginning of words
[8]   between voiced sounds
[9]   at the beginning of a syllable
[10] at the end of a syllable
[11] at the end of a syllable
[12] at the beginning of words
[13] between voiced sounds

ABBREVIATIONS
used in the vocabulary

English abbreviations

ab.	-	about
adj	-	adjective
adv	-	adverb
anim.	-	animate
as adj	-	attributive noun used as adjective
e.g.	-	for example
etc.	-	et cetera
fam.	-	familiar
fem.	-	feminine
form.	-	formal
inanim.	-	inanimate
masc.	-	masculine
math	-	mathematics
mil.	-	military
n	-	noun
pl	-	plural
pron.	-	pronoun
sb	-	somebody
sing.	-	singular
sth	-	something
v aux	-	auxiliary verb
vi	-	intransitive verb
vi, vt	-	intransitive, transitive verb
vt	-	transitive verb

BASIC CONCEPTS

Basic concepts. Part 1

1. Pronouns

I, me	나, 저	na
you	너	neo
he	그, 그분	geu, geu-bun
she	그녀	geu-nyeo
it	그것	geu-geot
we	우리	u-ri
you (to a group)	너희	neo-hui
you (polite, sing.)	당신	dang-sin
they	그들	geu-deul

2. Greetings. Salutations. Farewells

Hello! (fam.)	안녕!	an-nyeong!
Hello! (form.)	안녕하세요!	an-nyeong-ha-se-yo!
Good morning!	안녕하세요!	an-nyeong-ha-se-yo!
Good afternoon!	안녕하세요!	an-nyeong-ha-se-yo!
Good evening!	안녕하세요!	an-nyeong-ha-se-yo!
to say hello	인사하다	in-sa-ha-da
Hi! (hello)	안녕!	an-nyeong!
greeting (n)	인사	in-sa
to greet (vt)	인사하다	in-sa-ha-da
How are you?	잘 지내세요?	jal ji-nae-se-yo?
What's new?	어떻게 지내?	eo-tteo-ke ji-nae?
Bye-Bye! Goodbye!	안녕히 가세요!	an-nyeong-hi ga-se-yo!
See you soon!	또 만나요!	tto man-na-yo!
Farewell! (to a friend)	잘 있어!	jal ri-seo!
Farewell! (form.)	안녕히 계세요!	an-nyeong-hi gye-se-yo!
to say goodbye	작별인사를 하다	jak-byeo-rin-sa-reul ha-da
So long!	안녕!	an-nyeong!
Thank you!	감사합니다!	gam-sa-ham-ni-da!
Thank you very much!	대단히 감사합니다!	dae-dan-hi gam-sa-ham-ni-da!

| You're welcome | 천만이에요 | cheon-man-i-e-yo |
| Don't mention it! | 천만의 말씀입니다 | cheon-man-ui mal-sseum-im-ni-da |

It was nothing	천만에	cheon-man-e
Excuse me! (fam.)	실례!	sil-lye!
Excuse me! (form.)	실례합니다!	sil-lye-ham-ni-da!
to excuse (forgive)	용서하다	yong-seo-ha-da

to apologize (vi)	사과하다	sa-gwa-ha-da
My apologies	사과드립니다	sa-gwa-deu-rim-ni-da
I'm sorry!	죄송합니다!	joe-song-ham-ni-da!
to forgive (vt)	용서하다	yong-seo-ha-da
please (adv)	부탁합니다	bu-tak-am-ni-da

Don't forget!	잊지 마십시오!	it-ji ma-sip-si-o!
Certainly!	몰론이에요!	mul-lon-i-e-yo!
Of course not!	몰론 아니에요!	mul-lon a-ni-e-yo!
Okay! (I agree)	그래요!	geu-rae-yo!
That's enough!	그만!	geu-man!

3. How to address

mister, sir	선생	seon-saeng
ma'am	여사님	yeo-sa-nim
miss	아가씨	a-ga-ssi
young man	젊은 분	jeol-meun bun
young man (little boy, kid)	꼬마	kko-ma
miss (little girl)	꼬마	kko-ma

4. Cardinal numbers. Part 1

0 zero	영	yeong
1 one	일	il
2 two	이	i
3 three	삼	sam
4 four	사	sa

5 five	오	o
6 six	육	yuk
7 seven	칠	chil
8 eight	팔	pal
9 nine	구	gu

10 ten	십	sip
11 eleven	십일	si-bil
12 twelve	십이	si-bi
13 thirteen	십삼	sip-sam
14 fourteen	십사	sip-sa

15 fifteen	십오	si-bo
16 sixteen	십육	si-byuk
17 seventeen	십칠	sip-chil
18 eighteen	십팔	sip-pal
19 nineteen	십구	sip-gu
20 twenty	이십	i-sip
21 twenty-one	이십일	i-si-bil
22 twenty-two	이십이	i-si-bi
23 twenty-three	이십삼	i-sip-sam
30 thirty	삼십	sam-sip
31 thirty-one	삼십일	sam-si-bil
32 thirty-two	삼십이	sam-si-bi
33 thirty-three	삼십삼	sam-sip-sam
40 forty	사십	sa-sip
41 forty-one	사십일	sa-si-bil
42 forty-two	사십이	sa-si-bi
43 forty-three	사십삼	sa-sip-sam
50 fifty	오십	o-sip
51 fifty-one	오십일	o-si-bil
52 fifty-two	오십이	o-si-bi
53 fifty-three	오십삼	o-sip-sam
60 sixty	육십	yuk-sip
61 sixty-one	육십일	yuk-si-bil
62 sixty-two	육십이	yuk-si-bi
63 sixty-three	육십삼	yuk-sip-sam
70 seventy	칠십	chil-sip
71 seventy-one	칠십일	chil-si-bil
72 seventy-two	칠십이	chil-si-bi
73 seventy-three	칠십삼	chil-sip-sam
80 eighty	팔십	pal-sip
81 eighty-one	팔십일	pal-si-bil
82 eighty-two	팔십이	pal-si-bi
83 eighty-three	팔십삼	pal-sip-sam
90 ninety	구십	gu-sip
91 ninety-one	구십일	gu-si-bil
92 ninety-two	구십이	gu-si-bi
93 ninety-three	구십삼	gu-sip-sam

5. Cardinal numbers. Part 2

| 100 one hundred | 백 | baek |
| 200 two hundred | 이백 | i-baek |

300 three hundred	삼백	sam-baek
400 four hundred	사백	sa-baek
500 five hundred	오백	o-baek
600 six hundred	육백	yuk-baek
700 seven hundred	칠백	chil-baek
800 eight hundred	팔백	pal-baek
900 nine hundred	구백	gu-baek
1000 one thousand	천	cheon
2000 two thousand	이천	i-cheon
3000 three thousand	삼천	sam-cheon
10000 ten thousand	만	man
one hundred thousand	십만	sim-man
million	백만	baeng-man
billion	십억	si-beok

6. Ordinal numbers

first (adj)	첫 번째의	cheot beon-jjae-ui
second (adj)	두 번째의	du beon-jjae-ui
third (adj)	세 번째의	se beon-jjae-ui
fourth (adj)	네 번째의	ne beon-jjae-ui
fifth (adj)	다섯 번째의	da-seot beon-jjae-ui
sixth (adj)	여섯 번째의	yeo-seot beon-jjae-ui
seventh (adj)	일곱 번째의	il-gop beon-jjae-ui
eighth (adj)	여덟 번째의	yeo-deol beon-jjae-ui
ninth (adj)	아홉 번째의	a-hop beon-jjae-ui
tenth (adj)	열 번째의	yeol beon-jjae-ui

7. Numbers. Fractions

fraction	분수	bun-su
one half	이분의 일	i-bun-ui il
one third	삼분의 일	sam-bun-ui il
one quarter	사분의 일	sa-bun-ui il
one eighth	팔분의 일	pal-bun-ui il
one tenth	십분의 일	sip-bun-ui il
two thirds	삼분의 이	sam-bun-ui i
three quarters	사분의 삼	sa-bun-ui sam

8. Numbers. Basic operations

subtraction	빼기	ppae-gi
to subtract (vi, vt)	빼다	ppae-da

division	나누기	na-nu-gi
to divide (vt)	나누다	na-nu-da
addition	더하기	deo-ha-gi
to add up (vt)	합하다	ha-pa-da
to add (vi, vt)	더하다	deo-ha-da
multiplication	곱하기	go-pa-gi
to multiply (vt)	곱하다	go-pa-da

9. Numbers. Miscellaneous

digit, figure	숫자	sut-ja
number	숫자	sut-ja
numeral	수사	su-sa
minus sign	마이너스	ma-i-neo-seu
plus sign	플러스	peul-leo-seu
formula	공식	gong-sik
calculation	계산	gye-san
to count (vi, vt)	세다	se-da
to count up	헤아리다	he-a-ri-da
to compare (vt)	비교하다	bi-gyo-ha-da
How much?	얼마?	eol-ma?
How many?	얼마나?	eo-di-ro?
sum, total	총합	chong-hap
result	결과	gyeol-gwa
remainder	나머지	na-meo-ji
a few (e.g., ~ years ago)	몇	myeot
little (I had ~ time)	조금	jo-geum
the rest	나머지	na-meo-ji
one and a half	일과 이분의 일	il-gwa i-bun-ui il
dozen	다스	da-seu
in half (adv)	반으로	ba-neu-ro
equally (evenly)	균등하게	gyun-deung-ha-ge
half	절반	jeol-ban
time (three ~s)	번	beon

10. The most important verbs. Part 1

to advise (vt)	조언하다	jo-eon-ha-da
to agree (say yes)	동의하다	dong-ui-ha-da
to answer (vi, vt)	대답하다	dae-da-pa-da
to apologize (vi)	사과하다	sa-gwa-ha-da
to arrive (vi)	도착하다	do-chak-a-da
to ask (~ oneself)	묻다	mut-da

to ask (~ sb to do sth)	부탁하다	bu-tak-a-da
to be afraid	무서워하다	mu-seo-wo-ha-da
to be hungry	배가 고프다	bae-ga go-peu-da
to be interested in ...	… 에 관심을 가지다	… e gwan-si-meul ga-ji-da
to be needed	필요하다	pi-ryo-ha-da
to be surprised	놀라다	nol-la-da
to be thirsty	목마르다	mong-ma-reu-da
to begin (vt)	시작하다	si-jak-a-da
to belong to ...	… 에 속하다	… e sok-a-da
to boast (vi)	자랑하다	ja-rang-ha-da
to break (split into pieces)	깨뜨리다	kkae-tteu-ri-da
to call (~ for help)	부르다, 요청하다	bu-reu-da, yo-cheong-ha-da
can (v aux)	할 수 있다	hal su it-da
to catch (vt)	잡다	jap-da
to change (vt)	바꾸다	ba-kku-da
to choose (select)	선택하다	seon-taek-a-da
to come down (the stairs)	내려오다	nae-ryeo-o-da
to compare (vt)	비교하다	bi-gyo-ha-da
to complain (vi, vt)	불평하다	bul-pyeong-ha-da
to confuse (mix up)	혼동하다	hon-dong-ha-da
to continue (vt)	계속하다	gye-sok-a-da
to control (vt)	제어하다	je-eo-ha-da
to cook (dinner)	요리하다	yo-ri-ha-da
to cost (vt)	값이 … 이다	gap-si … i-da
to count (add up)	세다	se-da
to count on ...	… 에 의지하다	… e ui-ji-ha-da
to create (vt)	창조하다	chang-jo-ha-da
to cry (weep)	울다	ul-da

11. The most important verbs. Part 2

to deceive (vi, vt)	속이다	so-gi-da
to decorate (tree, street)	장식하다	jang-sik-a-da
to defend (a country, etc.)	방어하다	bang-eo-ha-da
to demand (request firmly)	요구하다	yo-gu-ha-da
to dig (vt)	파다	pa-da
to discuss (vt)	의논하다	ui-non-ha-da
to do (vt)	하다	ha-da
to doubt (have doubts)	의심하다	ui-sim-ha-da
to drop (let fall)	떨어뜨리다	tteo-reo-tteu-ri-da
to enter (room, house, etc.)	들어가다	deu-reo-ga-da
to exist (vi)	존재하다	jon-jae-ha-da
to expect (foresee)	예상하다	ye-sang-ha-da

to explain (vt)	설명하다	seol-myeong-ha-da
to fall (vi)	떨어지다	tteo-reo-ji-da
to find (vt)	찾다	chat-da
to finish (vt)	끝내다	kkeun-nae-da
to fly (vi)	날다	nal-da
to follow ... (come after)	··· 를 따라가다	... reul tta-ra-ga-da
to forget (vi, vt)	잊다	it-da
to forgive (vt)	용서하다	yong-seo-ha-da
to give (vt)	주다	ju-da
to give a hint	힌트를 주다	hin-teu-reul ju-da
to go (on foot)	가다	ga-da
to go for a swim	수영하다	su-yeong-ha-da
to go out (for dinner, etc.)	나가다	na-ga-da
to guess (the answer)	추측하다	chu-cheuk-a-da
to have (vt)	가지다	ga-ji-da
to have breakfast	아침을 먹다	a-chi-meul meok-da
to have dinner	저녁을 먹다	jeo-nyeo-geul meok-da
to have lunch	점심을 먹다	jeom-si-meul meok-da
to hear (vt)	듣다	deut-da
to help (vt)	도와주다	do-wa-ju-da
to hide (vt)	숨기다	sum-gi-da
to hope (vi, vt)	희망하다	hui-mang-ha-da
to hunt (vi, vt)	사냥하다	sa-nyang-ha-da
to hurry (vi)	서두르다	seo-du-reu-da

12. The most important verbs. Part 3

to inform (vt)	알리다	al-li-da
to insist (vi, vt)	주장하다	ju-jang-ha-da
to insult (vt)	모욕하다	mo-yok-a-da
to invite (vt)	초대하다	cho-dae-ha-da
to joke (vi)	농담하다	nong-dam-ha-da
to keep (vt)	보관하다	bo-gwan-ha-da
to keep silent	침묵을 지키다	chim-mu-geul ji-ki-da
to kill (vt)	죽이다	ju-gi-da
to know (sb)	알다	al-da
to know (sth)	알다	al-da
to laugh (vi)	웃다	ut-da
to liberate (city, etc.)	해방하다	hae-bang-ha-da
to like (I like ...)	좋아하다	jo-a-ha-da
to look for ... (search)	··· 를 찾다	... reul chat-da
to love (sb)	사랑하다	sa-rang-ha-da
to make a mistake	실수하다	sil-su-ha-da

to manage, to run	운영하다	u-nyeong-ha-da
to mean (signify)	의미하다	ui-mi-ha-da
to mention (talk about)	언급하다	eon-geu-pa-da
to miss (school, etc.)	결석하다	gyeol-seok-a-da
to notice (see)	알아차리다	a-ra-cha-ri-da
to object (vi, vt)	반대하다	ban-dae-ha-da
to observe (see)	지켜보다	ji-kyeo-bo-da
to open (vt)	열다	yeol-da
to order (meal, etc.)	주문하다	ju-mun-ha-da
to order (mil.)	명령하다	myeong-nyeong-ha-da
to own (possess)	소유하다	so-yu-ha-da
to participate (vi)	참가하다	cham-ga-ha-da
to pay (vi, vt)	지불하다	ji-bul-ha-da
to permit (vt)	허가하다	heo-ga-ha-da
to plan (vt)	계획하다	gye-hoek-a-da
to play (children)	놀다	nol-da
to pray (vi, vt)	기도하다	gi-do-ha-da
to prefer (vt)	선호하다	seon-ho-ha-da
to promise (vt)	약속하다	yak-sok-a-da
to pronounce (vt)	발음하다	ba-reum-ha-da
to propose (vt)	제안하다	je-an-ha-da
to punish (vt)	처벌하다	cheo-beol-ha-da

13. The most important verbs. Part 4

to read (vi, vt)	읽다	ik-da
to recommend (vt)	추천하다	chu-cheon-ha-da
to refuse (vi, vt)	거절하다	geo-jeol-ha-da
to regret (be sorry)	후회하다	hu-hoe-ha-da
to rent (sth from sb)	임대하다	im-dae-ha-da
to repeat (say again)	반복하다	ban-bok-a-da
to reserve, to book	예약하다	ye-yak-a-da
to run (vi)	달리다	dal-li-da
to save (rescue)	구조하다	gu-jo-ha-da
to say (~ thank you)	말하다	mal-ha-da
to scold (vt)	꾸짖다	kku-jit-da
to see (vt)	보다	bo-da
to sell (vt)	팔다	pal-da
to send (vt)	보내다	bo-nae-da
to shoot (vi)	쏘다	sso-da
to shout (vi)	소리치다	so-ri-chi-da
to show (vt)	보여주다	bo-yeo-ju-da
to sign (document)	서명하다	seo-myeong-ha-da
to sit down (vi)	앉다	an-da

to smile (vi)	미소를 짓다	mi-so-reul jit-da
to speak (vi, vt)	말하다	mal-ha-da
to steal (money, etc.)	훔치다	hum-chi-da
to stop (for pause, etc.)	정지하다	jeong-ji-ha-da
to stop (please ~ calling me)	그만두다	geu-man-du-da

to study (vt)	공부하다	gong-bu-ha-da
to swim (vi)	수영하다	su-yeong-ha-da
to take (vt)	잡다	jap-da
to think (vi, vt)	생각하다	saeng-gak-a-da
to threaten (vt)	협박하다	hyeop-bak-a-da

to touch (with hands)	닿다	da-ta
to translate (vt)	번역하다	beo-nyeok-a-da
to trust (vt)	신뢰하다	sil-loe-ha-da
to try (attempt)	해보다	hae-bo-da
to turn (e.g., ~ left)	돌다	dol-da

to underestimate (vt)	과소평가하다	gwa-so-pyeong-ga-ha-da
to understand (vt)	이해하다	i-hae-ha-da
to unite (vt)	연합하다	yeon-ha-pa-da
to wait (vt)	기다리다	gi-da-ri-da

to want (wish, desire)	원하다	won-ha-da
to warn (vt)	경고하다	gyeong-go-ha-da
to work (vi)	일하다	il-ha-da
to write (vt)	쓰다	sseu-da
to write down	적다	jeok-da

14. Colors

color	색	sae
shade (tint)	색조	saek-jo
hue	색상	saek-sang
rainbow	무지개	mu-ji-gae

white (adj)	흰	huin
black (adj)	검은	geo-meun
gray (adj)	회색의	hoe-sae-gui

green (adj)	초록색의	cho-rok-sae-gui
yellow (adj)	노란	no-ran
red (adj)	빨간	ppal-gan

blue (adj)	파란	pa-ran
light blue (adj)	하늘색의	ha-neul-sae-gui
pink (adj)	분홍색의	bun-hong-sae-gui
orange (adj)	주황색의	ju-hwang-sae-gui
violet (adj)	보라색의	bo-ra-sae-gui

brown (adj)	갈색의	gal-sae-gui
golden (adj)	금색의	geum-sae-gui
silvery (adj)	은색의	eun-sae-gui
beige (adj)	베이지색의	be-i-ji-sae-gui
cream (adj)	크림색의	keu-rim-sae-gui
turquoise (adj)	청록색의	cheong-nok-sae-gui
cherry red (adj)	암적색의	am-jeok-sae-gui
lilac (adj)	연보라색의	yeon-bo-ra-sae-gui
crimson (adj)	진홍색의	jin-hong-sae-gui
light (adj)	밝은	bal-geun
dark (adj)	짙은	ji-teun
bright, vivid (adj)	선명한	seon-myeong-han
colored (pencils)	색의	sae-gui
color (e.g., ~ film)	컬러의	keol-leo-ui
black-and-white (adj)	흑백의	heuk-bae-gui
plain (one-colored)	단색의	dan-sae-gui
multicolored (adj)	다색의	da-sae-gui

15. Questions

Who?	누구?	nu-gu?
What?	무엇?	mu-eot?
Where? (at, in)	어디?	eo-di?
Where? (to)?	어디로?	eo-di-ro?
From where?	어디로부터?	eo-di-ro-bu-teo?
When?	언제?	eon-je?
Why? (What for?)	왜?	wae?
Why? (~ are you crying?)	왜?	wae?
What for?	무엇을 위해서?	mu-eos-eul rwi-hae-seo?
How? (in what way)	어떻게?	eo-tteo-ke?
What? (What kind of ...?)	어떤?	eo-tteon?
Which?	어느?	eo-neu?
To whom?	누구에게?	nu-gu-e-ge?
About whom?	누구에 대하여?	nu-gu-e dae-ha-yeo?
About what?	무엇에 대하여?	mu-eos-e dae-ha-yeo?
With whom?	누구하고?	nu-gu-ha-go?
How many? How much?	얼마?	eol-ma?
Whose?	누구의?	nu-gu-ui?

16. Prepositions

with (accompanied by)	··· 하고	... ha-go
without	없이	eop-si

to (indicating direction)	··· 에	... e
about (talking ~ ...)	··· 에 대하여	... e dae-ha-yeo
before (in time)	전에	jeon-e
in front of ...	··· 앞에	... a-pe

under (beneath, below)	밑에	mi-te
above (over)	위에	wi-e
on (atop)	위에	wi-e
from (off, out of)	··· 에서	... e-seo
of (made from)	··· 로	... ro

| in (e.g., ~ ten minutes) | ··· 안에 | ... a-ne |
| over (across the top of) | 너머 | dwi-e |

17. Function words. Adverbs. Part 1

Where? (at, in)	어디?	eo-di?
here (adv)	여기	yeo-gi
there (adv)	거기	geo-gi

| somewhere (to be) | 어딘가 | eo-din-ga |
| nowhere (not anywhere) | 어디도 | eo-di-do |

| by (near, beside) | 옆에 | yeo-pe |
| by the window | 창문 옆에 | chang-mun nyeo-pe |

Where (to)?	어디로?	eo-di-ro?
here (e.g., come ~!)	여기로	yeo-gi-ro
there (e.g., to go ~)	거기로	geo-gi-ro
from here (adv)	여기서	yeo-gi-seo
from there (adv)	거기서	geo-gi-seo

| close (adv) | 가까이 | ga-kka-i |
| far (adv) | 멀리 | meol-li |

near (e.g., ~ Paris)	근처에	geun-cheo-e
nearby (adv)	인근에	in-geu-ne
not far (adv)	멀지 않게	meol-ji an-ke

left (adj)	왼쪽의	oen-jjo-gui
on the left	왼쪽에	oen-jjo-ge
to the left	왼쪽으로	oen-jjo-geu-ro

right (adj)	오른쪽의	o-reun-jjo-gui
on the right	오른쪽에	o-reun-jjo-ge
to the right	오른쪽으로	o-reun-jjo-geu-ro

in front (adv)	앞쪽에	ap-jjo-ge
front (as adj)	앞의	a-pui
ahead (the kids ran ~)	앞으로	a-peu-ro

behind (adv)	뒤에	dwi-e
from behind	뒤에서	dwi-e-seo
back (towards the rear)	뒤로	dwi-ro
middle	가운데	ga-un-de
in the middle	가운데에	ga-un-de-e
at the side	옆에	yeo-pe
everywhere (adv)	모든 곳에	mo-deun gos-e
around (in all directions)	주위에	ju-wi-e
from inside	내면에서	nae-myeon-e-seo
somewhere (to go)	어딘가에	eo-din-ga-e
straight (directly)	똑바로	ttok-ba-ro
back (e.g., come ~)	뒤로	dwi-ro
from anywhere	어디에서든지	eo-di-e-seo-deun-ji
from somewhere	어디로부터인지	eo-di-ro-bu-teo-in-ji
firstly (adv)	첫째로	cheot-jjae-ro
secondly (adv)	둘째로	dul-jjae-ro
thirdly (adv)	셋째로	set-jjae-ro
suddenly (adv)	갑자기	gap-ja-gi
at first (in the beginning)	처음에	cheo-eum-e
for the first time	처음으로	cheo-eu-meu-ro
long before ...	··· 오래 전에	... o-rae jeon-e
anew (over again)	다시	da-si
for good (adv)	영원히	yeong-won-hi
never (adv)	절대로	jeol-dae-ro
again (adv)	다시	da-si
now (adv)	이제	i-je
often (adv)	자주	ja-ju
then (adv)	그때	geu-ttae
urgently (quickly)	급히	geu-pi
usually (adv)	보통으로	bo-tong-eu-ro
by the way, ...	그건 그렇고, ···	geu-geon geu-reo-ko, ...
possible (that is ~)	가능한	ga-neung-han
probably (adv)	아마	a-ma
maybe (adv)	어쩌면	eo-jjeo-myeon
besides ...	게다가 ···	ge-da-ga ...
that's why ...	그래서 ···	geu-rae-seo ...
in spite of ...	··· 에도 불구하고	... e-do bul-gu-ha-go
thanks to ...	··· 덕분에	... deok-bun-e
something	무엇인가	mu-eon-nin-ga
anything (something)	무엇이든지	mu-eon-ni-deun-ji
nothing	아무것도	a-mu-geot-do
someone	누구	nu-gu
somebody	누군가	nu-gun-ga

nobody	아무도	a-mu-do
nowhere (a voyage to ~)	아무데도	a-mu-de-do
nobody's	누구의 것도 아닌	nu-gu-ui geot-do a-nin
somebody's	누군가의	nu-gun-ga-ui

so (I'm ~ glad)	그래서	geu-rae-seo
also (as well)	역시	yeok-si
too (as well)	또한	tto-han

18. Function words. Adverbs. Part 2

Why?	왜?	wae?
for some reason	어떤 이유로	eo-tteon ni-yu-ro
because ...	왜냐하면 ···	wae-nya-ha-myeon ...
for some purpose	어떤 목적으로	eo-tteon mok-jeo-geu-ro

and	그리고	geu-ri-go
or	또는	tto-neun
but	그러나	geu-reo-na
for (e.g., ~ me)	위해서	wi-hae-seo

too (~ many people)	너무	neo-mu
only (exclusively)	··· 만	... man
exactly (adv)	정확하게	jeong-hwak-a-ge
about (more or less)	약	yak

approximately (adv)	대략	dae-ryak
approximate (adj)	대략적인	dae-ryak-jeo-gin
almost (adv)	거의	geo-ui
the rest	나머지	na-meo-ji

each (adj)	각각의	gak-ga-gui
any (no matter which)	아무	a-mu
many, much (a lot of)	많이	ma-ni
many people	많은 사람들	ma-neun sa-ram-deul
all (everyone)	모두	mo-du

in return for ...	··· 의 교환으로	... ui gyo-hwa-neu-ro
in exchange (adv)	교환으로	gyo-hwa-neu-ro
by hand (made)	수공으로	su-gong-eu-ro
hardly (negative opinion)	거의	geo-ui

probably (adv)	아마	a-ma
on purpose (intentionally)	일부러	il-bu-reo
by accident (adv)	우연히	u-yeon-hi

very (adv)	아주	a-ju
for example (adv)	예를 들면	ye-reul deul-myeon
between	사이에	sa-i-e
among	중에	jung-e

so much (such a lot)	이만큼	i-man-keum
especially (adv)	특히	teuk-i

Basic concepts. Part 2

19. Weekdays

Monday	월요일	wo-ryo-il
Tuesday	화요일	hwa-yo-il
Wednesday	수요일	su-yo-il
Thursday	목요일	mo-gyo-il
Friday	금요일	geu-myo-il
Saturday	토요일	to-yo-il
Sunday	일요일	i-ryo-il
today (adv)	오늘	o-neul
tomorrow (adv)	내일	nae-il
the day after tomorrow	모레	mo-re
yesterday (adv)	어제	eo-je
the day before yesterday	그저께	geu-jeo-kke
day	낮	nat
working day	근무일	geun-mu-il
public holiday	공휴일	gong-hyu-il
day off	휴일	hyu-il
weekend	주말	ju-mal
all day long	하루종일	ha-ru-jong-il
the next day (adv)	다음날	da-eum-nal
two days ago	이틀 전	i-teul jeon
the day before	전날	jeon-nal
daily (adj)	일간의	il-ga-nui
every day (adv)	매일	mae-il
week	주	ju
last week (adv)	지난 주에	ji-nan ju-e
next week (adv)	다음 주에	da-eum ju-e
weekly (adj)	주간의	ju-ga-nui
every week (adv)	매주	mae-ju
twice a week	일주일에 두번	il-ju-i-re du-beon
every Tuesday	매주 화요일	mae-ju hwa-yo-il

20. Hours. Day and night

morning	아침	a-chim
in the morning	아침에	a-chim-e
noon, midday	정오	jeong-o

in the afternoon	오후에	o-hu-e
evening	저녁	jeo-nyeok
in the evening	저녁에	jeo-nyeo-ge
night	밤	bam
at night	밤에	bam-e
midnight	자정	ja-jeong
second	초	cho
minute	분	bun
hour	시	si
half an hour	반시간	ban-si-gan
a quarter-hour	십오분	si-bo-bun
fifteen minutes	십오분	si-bo-bun
24 hours	이십사시간	i-sip-sa-si-gan
sunrise	일출	il-chul
dawn	새벽	sae-byeok
early morning	이른 아침	i-reun a-chim
sunset	저녁 노을	jeo-nyeok no-eul
early in the morning	이른 아침에	i-reun a-chim-e
this morning	오늘 아침에	o-neul ra-chim-e
tomorrow morning	내일 아침에	nae-il ra-chim-e
this afternoon	오늘 오후에	o-neul ro-hu-e
in the afternoon	오후에	o-hu-e
tomorrow afternoon	내일 오후에	nae-il ro-hu-e
tonight (this evening)	오늘 저녁에	o-neul jeo-nyeo-ge
tomorrow night	내일 밤에	nae-il bam-e
at 3 o'clock sharp	3시 정각에	se-si jeong-ga-ge
about 4 o'clock	4시쯤에	ne-si-jjeu-me
by 12 o'clock	12시까지	yeoldu si-kka-ji
in 20 minutes	20분 안에	isib-bun na-ne
in an hour	한 시간 안에	han si-gan na-ne
on time (adv)	제시간에	je-si-gan-e
a quarter of ...	… 십오 분	… si-bo bun
within an hour	한 시간 내에	han si-gan nae-e
every 15 minutes	15분 마다	sibo-bun ma-da
round the clock	하루종일	ha-ru-jong-il

21. Months. Seasons

January	일월	i-rwol
February	이월	i-wol
March	삼월	sam-wol
April	사월	sa-wol

May	오월	o-wol
June	유월	yu-wol
July	칠월	chi-rwol
August	팔월	pa-rwol
September	구월	gu-wol
October	시월	si-wol
November	십일월	si-bi-rwol
December	십이월	si-bi-wol
spring	봄	bom
in spring	봄에	bom-e
spring (as adj)	봄의	bom-ui
summer	여름	yeo-reum
in summer	여름에	yeo-reum-e
summer (as adj)	여름의	yeo-reu-mui
fall	가을	ga-eul
in fall	가을에	ga-eu-re
fall (as adj)	가을의	ga-eu-rui
winter	겨울	gyeo-ul
in winter	겨울에	gyeo-u-re
winter (as adj)	겨울의	gyeo-ul
month	월, 달	wol, dal
this month	이번 달에	i-beon da-re
next month	다음 달에	da-eum da-re
last month	지난 달에	ji-nan da-re
a month ago	한달 전에	han-dal jeon-e
in a month (a month later)	한 달 안에	han dal ra-ne
in 2 months (2 months later)	두 달 안에	du dal ra-ne
the whole month	한 달 내내	han dal lae-nae
all month long	한달간 내내	han-dal-gan nae-nae
monthly (~ magazine)	월간의	wol-ga-nui
monthly (adv)	매월, 매달	mae-wol, mae-dal
every month	매달	mae-dal
twice a month	한 달에 두 번	han da-re du beon
year	년	nyeon
this year	올해	ol-hae
next year	내년	nae-nyeon
last year	작년	jang-nyeon
a year ago	일년 전	il-lyeon jeon
in a year	일 년 안에	il lyeon na-ne
in two years	이 년 안에	i nyeon na-ne
the whole year	한 해 전체	han hae jeon-che

all year long	일년 내내	il-lyeon nae-nae
every year	매년	mae-nyeon
annual (adj)	연간의	yeon-ga-nui
annually (adv)	매년	mae-nyeon
4 times a year	일년에 네 번	il-lyeon-e ne beon

date (e.g., today's ~)	날짜	nal-jja
date (e.g., ~ of birth)	월일	wo-ril
calendar	달력	dal-lyeok

half a year	반년	ban-nyeon
six months	육개월	yuk-gae-wol
season (summer, etc.)	계절	gye-jeol
century	세기	se-gi

22. Units of measurement

weight	무게	mu-ge
length	길이	gi-ri
width	폭, 너비	pok, neo-bi
height	높이	no-pi
depth	깊이	gi-pi
volume	부피	bu-pi
area	면적	myeon-jeok

gram	그램	geu-raem
milligram	밀리그램	mil-li-geu-raem
kilogram	킬로그램	kil-lo-geu-raem
ton	톤	ton
pound	파운드	pa-un-deu
ounce	온스	on-seu

meter	미터	mi-teo
millimeter	밀리미터	mil-li-mi-teo
centimeter	센티미터	sen-ti-mi-teo
kilometer	킬로미터	kil-lo-mi-teo
mile	마일	ma-il

inch	인치	in-chi
foot	피트	pi-teu
yard	야드	ya-deu

| square meter | 제곱미터 | je-gom-mi-teo |
| hectare | 헥타르 | hek-ta-reu |

liter	리터	ri-teo
degree	도	do
volt	볼트	bol-teu
ampere	암페어	am-pe-eo
horsepower	마력	ma-ryeok

quantity	수량, 양	su-ryang, yang
a little bit of ...	... 조금	... jo-geum
half	절반	jeol-ban
dozen	다스	da-seu
piece (item)	조각	jo-gak

| size | 크기 | keu-gi |
| scale (map ~) | 축척 | chuk-cheok |

minimal (adj)	최소의	choe-so-ui
the smallest (adj)	가장 작은	ga-jang ja-geun
medium (adj)	중간의	jung-gan-ui
maximal (adj)	최대의	choe-dae-ui
the largest (adj)	가장 큰	ga-jang keun

23. Containers

canning jar (glass ~)	유리병	yu-ri-byeong
can	캔, 깡통	kaen, kkang-tong
bucket	양동이	yang-dong-i
barrel	통	tong

wash basin (e.g., plastic ~)	대야	dae-ya
tank (100L water ~)	탱크	taeng-keu
hip flask	휴대용 술병	hyu-dae-yong sul-byeong
jerrycan	통	tong
tank (e.g., tank car)	탱크	taeng-keu

mug	머그컵	meo-geu-keop
cup (of coffee, etc.)	컵	keop
saucer	받침 접시	bat-chim jeop-si
glass (tumbler)	유리잔	yu-ri-jan
wine glass	와인글라스	wa-in-geul-la-seu
stock pot (soup pot)	냄비	naem-bi

| bottle (~ of wine) | 병 | byeong |
| neck (of the bottle, etc.) | 병목 | byeong-mok |

carafe (decanter)	디캔터	di-kaen-teo
pitcher	물병	mul-byeong
vessel (container)	용기	yong-gi
pot (crock, stoneware ~)	항아리	hang-a-ri
vase	화병	hwa-byeong

bottle (perfume ~)	향수병	hyang-su-byeong
vial, small bottle	약병	yak-byeong
tube (of toothpaste)	튜브	tyu-beu

| sack (bag) | 자루 | ja-ru |
| bag (paper ~, plastic ~) | 봉투 | bong-tu |

pack (of cigarettes, etc.)	갑	gap
box (e.g., shoebox)	박스	bak-seu
crate	상자	sang-ja
basket	바구니	ba-gu-ni

HUMAN BEING

Human being. The body

24. Head

head	머리	meo-ri
face	얼굴	eol-gul
nose	코	ko
mouth	입	ip
eye	눈	nun
eyes	눈	nun
pupil	눈동자	nun-dong-ja
eyebrow	눈썹	nun-sseop
eyelash	속눈썹	song-nun-sseop
eyelid	눈꺼풀	nun-kkeo-pul
tongue	혀	hyeo
tooth	이	i
lips	입술	ip-sul
cheekbones	광대뼈	gwang-dae-ppyeo
gum	잇몸	in-mom
palate	입천장	ip-cheon-jang
nostrils	콧구멍	kot-gu-meong
chin	턱	teok
jaw	턱	teok
cheek	뺨, 볼	ppyam, bol
forehead	이마	i-ma
temple	관자놀이	gwan-ja-no-ri
ear	귀	gwi
back of the head	뒤통수	dwi-tong-su
neck	목	mok
throat	목구멍	mok-gu-meong
hair	머리털, 헤어	meo-ri-teol, he-eo
hairstyle	머리 스타일	meo-ri seu-ta-il
haircut	헤어컷	he-eo-keot
wig	가발	ga-bal
mustache	콧수염	kot-su-yeom
beard	턱수염	teok-su-yeom
to have (a beard, etc.)	기르다	gi-reu-da

braid	땋은 머리	tta-eun meo-ri
sideburns	구레나룻	gu-re-na-rut
red-haired (adj)	빨강머리의	ppal-gang-meo-ri-ui
gray (hair)	흰머리의	huin-meo-ri-ui
bald (adj)	대머리인	dae-meo-ri-in
bald patch	땜통	ttaem-tong
ponytail	말총머리	mal-chong-meo-ri
bangs	앞머리	am-meo-ri

25. Human body

hand	손	son
arm	팔	pal
finger	손가락	son-ga-rak
thumb	엄지손가락	eom-ji-son-ga-rak
little finger	새끼손가락	sae-kki-son-ga-rak
nail	손톱	son-top
fist	주먹	ju-meok
palm	손바닥	son-ba-dak
wrist	손목	son-mok
forearm	전박	jeon-bak
elbow	팔꿈치	pal-kkum-chi
shoulder	어깨	eo-kkae
leg	다리	da-ri
foot	발	bal
knee	무릎	mu-reup
calf (part of leg)	종아리	jong-a-ri
hip	엉덩이	eong-deong-i
heel	발뒤꿈치	bal-dwi-kkum-chi
body	몸	mom
stomach	배	bae
chest	가슴	ga-seum
breast	가슴	ga-seum
flank	옆구리	yeop-gu-ri
back	등	deung
lower back	허리	heo-ri
waist	허리	heo-ri
navel (belly button)	배꼽	bae-kkop
buttocks	엉덩이	eong-deong-i
bottom	엉덩이	eong-deong-i
beauty mark	점	jeom
birthmark (café au lait spot)	모반	mo-ban

| tattoo | 문신 | mun-sin |
| scar | 흉터 | hyung-teo |

Clothing & Accessories

26. Outerwear. Coats

clothes	옷	ot
outerwear	겉옷	geo-tot
winter clothing	겨울옷	gyeo-u-rot

coat (overcoat)	코트	ko-teu
fur coat	모피 외투	mo-pi oe-tu
fur jacket	짧은 모피 외투	jjal-beun mo-pi oe-tu
down coat	패딩점퍼	pae-ding-jeom-peo

jacket (e.g., leather ~)	재킷	jae-kit
raincoat (trenchcoat, etc.)	트렌치코트	teu-ren-chi-ko-teu
waterproof (adj)	방수의	bang-su-ui

27. Men's & women's clothing

shirt (button shirt)	셔츠	syeo-cheu
pants	바지	ba-ji
jeans	청바지	cheong-ba-ji
suit jacket	재킷	jae-kit
suit	양복	yang-bok

dress (frock)	드레스	deu-re-seu
skirt	치마	chi-ma
blouse	블라우스	beul-la-u-seu
knitted jacket (cardigan, etc.)	니트 재킷	ni-teu jae-kit
jacket (of woman's suit)	재킷	jae-kit

T-shirt	티셔츠	ti-syeo-cheu
shorts (short trousers)	반바지	ban-ba-ji
tracksuit	운동복	un-dong-bok
bathrobe	목욕가운	mo-gyok-ga-un
pajamas	파자마	pa-ja-ma

| sweater | 스웨터 | seu-we-teo |
| pullover | 풀오버 | pu-ro-beo |

vest	조끼	jo-kki
tailcoat	연미복	yeon-mi-bok
tuxedo	턱시도	teok-si-do

uniform	제복	je-bok
workwear	작업복	ja-geop-bok
overalls	작업바지	ja-geop-ba-ji
coat (e.g., doctor's smock)	가운	ga-un

28. Clothing. Underwear

underwear	속옷	so-got
undershirt (A-shirt)	러닝 셔츠	reo-ning syeo-cheu
socks	양말	yang-mal
nightgown	잠옷	jam-ot
bra	브라	beu-ra
knee highs (knee-high socks)	무릎길이 스타킹	mu-reup-gi-ri seu-ta-king
pantyhose	팬티 스타킹	paen-ti seu-ta-king
stockings (thigh highs)	밴드 스타킹	baen-deu seu-ta-king
bathing suit	수영복	su-yeong-bok

29. Headwear

hat	모자	mo-ja
fedora	중절모	jung-jeol-mo
baseball cap	야구 모자	ya-gu mo-ja
flatcap	플랫캡	peul-laet-kaep
beret	베레모	be-re-mo
hood	후드	hu-deu
panama hat	파나마 모자	pa-na-ma mo-ja
knit cap (knitted hat)	니트 모자	ni-teu mo-ja
headscarf	스카프	seu-ka-peu
women's hat	여성용 모자	yeo-seong-yong mo-ja
hard hat	안전모	an-jeon-mo
garrison cap	개리슨 캡	gae-ri-seun kaep
helmet	헬멧	hel-met

30. Footwear

footwear	신발	sin-bal
shoes (men's shoes)	구두	gu-du
shoes (women's shoes)	구두	gu-du
boots (e.g., cowboy ~)	부츠	bu-cheu
slippers	슬리퍼	seul-li-peo
tennis shoes (e.g., Nike ~)	운동화	un-dong-hwa

sneakers (e.g., Converse ~)	스니커즈	seu-ni-keo-jeu
sandals	샌들	saen-deul

cobbler (shoe repairer)	구둣방	gu-dut-bang
heel	굽	gup
pair (of shoes)	켤레	kyeol-le

shoestring	끈	kkeun
to lace (vt)	끈을 매다	kkeu-neul mae-da
shoehorn	구둣주걱	gu-dut-ju-geok
shoe polish	구두약	gu-du-yak

31. Personal accessories

gloves	장갑	jang-gap
mittens	벙어리장갑	beong-eo-ri-jang-gap
scarf (muffler)	목도리	mok-do-ri

glasses (eyeglasses)	안경	an-gyeong
frame (eyeglass ~)	안경테	an-gyeong-te
umbrella	우산	u-san
walking stick	지팡이	ji-pang-i
hairbrush	빗, 솔빗	bit, sol-bit
fan	부채	bu-chae

tie (necktie)	넥타이	nek-ta-i
bow tie	나비넥타이	na-bi-nek-ta-i
suspenders	멜빵	mel-ppang
handkerchief	손수건	son-su-geon

comb	빗	bit
barrette	머리핀	meo-ri-pin
hairpin	머리핀	meo-ri-pin
buckle	버클	beo-keul

belt	벨트	bel-teu
shoulder strap	어깨끈	eo-kkae-kkeun

bag (handbag)	가방	ga-bang
purse	핸드백	haen-deu-baek
backpack	배낭	bae-nang

32. Clothing. Miscellaneous

fashion	패션	pae-syeon
in vogue (adj)	유행하는	yu-haeng-ha-neun
fashion designer	패션 디자이너	pae-syeon di-ja-i-neo

collar	옷깃	ot-git
pocket	주머니, 포켓	ju-meo-ni, po-ket
pocket (as adj)	주머니의	ju-meo-ni-ui
sleeve	소매	so-mae
hanging loop	거는 끈	geo-neun kkeun
fly (on trousers)	바지 지퍼	ba-ji ji-peo

zipper (fastener)	지퍼	ji-peo
fastener	조임쇠	jo-im-soe
button	단추	dan-chu
buttonhole	단춧 구멍	dan-chut gu-meong
to come off (ab. button)	떨어지다	tteo-reo-ji-da

to sew (vi, vt)	바느질하다	ba-neu-jil-ha-da
to embroider (vi, vt)	수놓다	su-no-ta
embroidery	자수	ja-su
sewing needle	바늘	ba-neul
thread	실	sil
seam	솔기	sol-gi

to get dirty (vi)	더러워지다	deo-reo-wo-ji-da
stain (mark, spot)	얼룩	eol-luk
to crease, crumple (vi)	구겨지다	gu-gyeo-ji-da
to tear, to rip (vt)	찢다	jjit-da
clothes moth	좀	jom

33. Personal care. Cosmetics

toothpaste	치약	chi-yak
toothbrush	칫솔	chit-sol
to brush one's teeth	이를 닦다	i-reul dak-da

razor	면도기	myeon-do-gi
shaving cream	면도용 크림	myeon-do-yong keu-rim
to shave (vi)	깎다	kkak-da

| soap | 비누 | bi-nu |
| shampoo | 샴푸 | syam-pu |

scissors	가위	ga-wi
nail file	손톱줄	son-top-jul
nail clippers	손톱깎이	son-top-kka-kki
tweezers	족집게	jok-jip-ge

cosmetics	화장품	hwa-jang-pum
face mask	얼굴 마스크	eol-gul ma-seu-keu
manicure	매니큐어	mae-ni-kyu-eo
to have a manicure	매니큐어를 칠하다	mae-ni-kyu-eo-reul chil-ha-da
pedicure	페디큐어	pe-di-kyu-eo

make-up bag	화장품 가방	hwa-jang-pum ga-bang
face powder	분	bun
powder compact	콤팩트	kom-paek-teu
blusher	블러셔	beul-leo-syeo

perfume (bottled)	향수	hyang-su
toilet water (lotion)	화장수	hwa-jang-su
lotion	로션	ro-syeon
cologne	오드콜로뉴	o-deu-kol-lo-nyu

eyeshadow	아이섀도	a-i-syae-do
eyeliner	아이라이너	a-i-ra-i-neo
mascara	마스카라	ma-seu-ka-ra

lipstick	립스틱	rip-seu-tik
nail polish, enamel	매니큐어	mae-ni-kyu-eo
hair spray	헤어 스프레이	he-eo seu-peu-re-i
deodorant	데오도란트	de-o-do-ran-teu

cream	크림	keu-rim
face cream	얼굴 크림	eol-gul keu-rim
hand cream	핸드 크림	haen-deu keu-rim
anti-wrinkle cream	주름제거 크림	ju-reum-je-geo keu-rim
day (as adj)	낮의	na-jui
night (as adj)	밤의	ba-mui

tampon	탐폰	tam-pon
toilet paper (toilet roll)	화장지	hwa-jang-ji
hair dryer	헤어 드라이어	he-eo deu-ra-i-eo

34. Watches. Clocks

watch (wristwatch)	손목 시계	son-mok si-gye
dial	문자반	mun-ja-ban
hand (of clock, watch)	바늘	ba-neul
metal watch band	금속제 시계줄	geum-sok-je si-gye-jul
watch strap	시계줄	si-gye-jul

battery	건전지	geon-jeon-ji
to be dead (battery)	나가다	na-ga-da
to change a battery	배터리를 갈다	bae-teo-ri-reul gal-da
to run fast	빨리 가다	ppal-li ga-da
to run slow	늦게 가다	neut-ge ga-da

wall clock	벽시계	byeok-si-gye
hourglass	모래시계	mo-rae-si-gye
sundial	해시계	hae-si-gye
alarm clock	알람 시계	al-lam si-gye
watchmaker	시계 기술자	si-gye gi-sul-ja
to repair (vt)	수리하다	su-ri-ha-da

Food. Nutricion

35. Food

meat	고기	go-gi
chicken	닭고기	dak-go-gi
Rock Cornish hen (poussin)	영계	yeong-gye
duck	오리고기	o-ri-go-gi
goose	거위고기	geo-wi-go-gi
game	사냥감	sa-nyang-gam
turkey	칠면조고기	chil-myeon-jo-go-gi
pork	돼지고기	dwae-ji-go-gi
veal	송아지 고기	song-a-ji go-gi
lamb	양고기	yang-go-gi
beef	소고기	so-go-gi
rabbit	토끼고기	to-kki-go-gi
sausage (bologna, pepperoni, etc.)	소시지	so-si-ji
vienna sausage (frankfurter)	비엔나 소시지	bi-en-na so-si-ji
bacon	베이컨	be-i-keon
ham	햄	haem
gammon	개먼	gae-meon
pâté	파테	pa-te
liver	간	gan
hamburger (ground beef)	다진 고기	da-jin go-gi
tongue	혀	hyeo
egg	계란	gye-ran
eggs	계란	gye-ran
egg white	흰자	huin-ja
egg yolk	노른자	no-reun-ja
fish	생선	saeng-seon
seafood	해물	hae-mul
caviar	캐비어	kae-bi-eo
crab	게	ge
shrimp	새우	sae-u
oyster	굴	gul
spiny lobster	대하	dae-ha
octopus	문어	mun-eo

squid	오징어	o-jing-eo
sturgeon	철갑상어	cheol-gap-sang-eo
salmon	연어	yeon-eo
halibut	넙치	neop-chi
cod	대구	dae-gu
mackerel	고등어	go-deung-eo
tuna	참치	cham-chi
eel	뱀장어	baem-jang-eo
trout	송어	song-eo
sardine	정어리	jeong-eo-ri
pike	강꼬치고기	gang-kko-chi-go-gi
herring	청어	cheong-eo
bread	빵	ppang
cheese	치즈	chi-jeu
sugar	설탕	seol-tang
salt	소금	so-geum
rice	쌀	ssal
pasta (macaroni)	파스타	pa-seu-ta
noodles	면	myeon
butter	버터	beo-teo
vegetable oil	식물유	sing-mu-ryu
sunflower oil	해바라기유	hae-ba-ra-gi-yu
margarine	마가린	ma-ga-rin
olives	올리브	ol-li-beu
olive oil	올리브유	ol-li-beu-yu
milk	우유	u-yu
condensed milk	연유	yeo-nyu
yogurt	요구르트	yo-gu-reu-teu
sour cream	사워크림	sa-wo-keu-rim
cream (of milk)	크림	keu-rim
mayonnaise	마요네즈	ma-yo-ne-jeu
buttercream	버터크림	beo-teo-keu-rim
cereal grains (wheat, etc.)	곡물	gong-mul
flour	밀가루	mil-ga-ru
canned food	통조림	tong-jo-rim
cornflakes	콘플레이크	kon-peul-le-i-keu
honey	꿀	kkul
jam	잼	jaem
chewing gum	껌	kkeom

36. Drinks

water	물	mul
drinking water	음료수	eum-nyo-su
mineral water	미네랄 워터	mi-ne-ral rwo-teo

still (adj)	탄산 없는	tan-san neom-neun
carbonated (adj)	탄산의	tan-sa-nui
sparkling (adj)	탄산이 든	tan-san-i deun
ice	얼음	eo-reum
with ice	얼음을 넣은	eo-reu-meul leo-eun

non-alcoholic (adj)	무알코올의	mu-al-ko-o-rui
soft drink	청량음료	cheong-nyang-eum-nyo
refreshing drink	청량 음료	cheong-nyang eum-nyo
lemonade	레모네이드	re-mo-ne-i-deu

liquors	술	sul
wine	와인	wa-in
white wine	백 포도주	baek po-do-ju
red wine	레드 와인	re-deu wa-in

liqueur	리큐르	ri-kyu-reu
champagne	샴페인	syam-pe-in
vermouth	베르무트	be-reu-mu-teu

whiskey	위스키	wi-seu-ki
vodka	보드카	bo-deu-ka
gin	진	jin
cognac	코냑	ko-nyak
rum	럼	reom

coffee	커피	keo-pi
black coffee	블랙 커피	beul-laek keo-pi
coffee with milk	밀크 커피	mil-keu keo-pi
cappuccino	카푸치노	ka-pu-chi-no
instant coffee	인스턴트 커피	in-seu-teon-teu keo-pi

milk	우유	u-yu
cocktail	칵테일	kak-te-il
milkshake	밀크 셰이크	mil-keu sye-i-keu

juice	주스	ju-seu
tomato juice	토마토 주스	to-ma-to ju-seu
orange juice	오렌지 주스	o-ren-ji ju-seu
freshly squeezed juice	생과일주스	saeng-gwa-il-ju-seu

beer	맥주	maek-ju
light beer	라거	ra-geo
dark beer	흑맥주	heung-maek-ju
tea	차	cha

| black tea | 홍차 | hong-cha |
| green tea | 녹차 | nok-cha |

37. Vegetables

| vegetables | 채소 | chae-so |
| greens | 녹황색 채소 | nok-wang-saek chae-so |

tomato	토마토	to-ma-to
cucumber	오이	o-i
carrot	당근	dang-geun
potato	감자	gam-ja
onion	양파	yang-pa
garlic	마늘	ma-neul

cabbage	양배추	yang-bae-chu
cauliflower	컬리플라워	keol-li-peul-la-wo
Brussels sprouts	방울다다기 양배추	bang-ul-da-da-gi yang-bae-chu
broccoli	브로콜리	beu-ro-kol-li

beetroot	비트	bi-teu
eggplant	가지	ga-ji
zucchini	애호박	ae-ho-bak
pumpkin	호박	ho-bak
turnip	순무	sun-mu

parsley	파슬리	pa-seul-li
dill	딜	dil
lettuce	양상추	yang-sang-chu
celery	셀러리	sel-leo-ri
asparagus	아스파라거스	a-seu-pa-ra-geo-seu
spinach	시금치	si-geum-chi

pea	완두	wan-du
beans	콩	kong
corn (maize)	옥수수	ok-su-su
kidney bean	강낭콩	gang-nang-kong

bell pepper	피망	pi-mang
radish	무	mu
artichoke	아티초크	a-ti-cho-keu

38. Fruits. Nuts

fruit	과일	gwa-il
apple	사과	sa-gwa
pear	배	bae

lemon	레몬	re-mon
orange	오렌지	o-ren-ji
strawberry (garden ~)	딸기	ttal-gi
mandarin	귤	gyul
plum	자두	ja-du
peach	복숭아	bok-sung-a
apricot	살구	sal-gu
raspberry	라즈베리	ra-jeu-be-ri
pineapple	파인애플	pa-in-ae-peul
banana	바나나	ba-na-na
watermelon	수박	su-bak
grape	포도	po-do
sour cherry	신양	si-nyang
sweet cherry	양벚나무	yang-beon-na-mu
melon	멜론	mel-lon
grapefruit	자몽	ja-mong
avocado	아보카도	a-bo-ka-do
papaya	파파야	pa-pa-ya
mango	망고	mang-go
pomegranate	석류	seong-nyu
redcurrant	레드커런트	re-deu-keo-ren-teu
blackcurrant	블랙커런트	beul-laek-keo-ren-teu
gooseberry	구스베리	gu-seu-be-ri
bilberry	빌베리	bil-be-ri
blackberry	블랙베리	beul-laek-be-ri
raisin	건포도	geon-po-do
fig	무화과	mu-hwa-gwa
date	대추야자	dae-chu-ya-ja
peanut	땅콩	ttang-kong
almond	아몬드	a-mon-deu
walnut	호두	ho-du
hazelnut	개암	gae-am
coconut	코코넛	ko-ko-neot
pistachios	피스타치오	pi-seu-ta-chi-o

39. Bread. Candy

bakers' confectionery (pastry)	과자류	gwa-ja-ryu
bread	빵	ppang
cookies	쿠키	ku-ki
chocolate (n)	초콜릿	cho-kol-lit
chocolate (as adj)	초콜릿의	cho-kol-lis-ui

candy (wrapped)	사탕	sa-tang
cake (e.g., cupcake)	케이크	ke-i-keu
cake (e.g., birthday ~)	케이크	ke-i-keu
pie (e.g., apple ~)	파이	pa-i
filling (for cake, pie)	속	sok
jam (whole fruit jam)	잼	jaem
marmalade	마멀레이드	ma-meol-le-i-deu
waffles	와플	wa-peul
ice-cream	아이스크림	a-i-seu-keu-rim

40. Cooked dishes

course, dish	요리, 코스	yo-ri, ko-seu
cuisine	요리	yo-ri
recipe	요리법	yo-ri-beop
portion	분량	bul-lyang
salad	샐러드	sael-leo-deu
soup	수프	su-peu
clear soup (broth)	육수	yuk-su
sandwich (bread)	샌드위치	saen-deu-wi-chi
fried eggs	계란후라이	gye-ran-hu-ra-i
hamburger (beefburger)	햄버거	haem-beo-geo
beefsteak	비프스테이크	bi-peu-seu-te-i-keu
side dish	사이드 메뉴	sa-i-deu me-nyu
spaghetti	스파게티	seu-pa-ge-ti
mashed potatoes	으깬 감자	eu-kkaen gam-ja
pizza	피자	pi-ja
porridge (oatmeal, etc.)	죽	juk
omelet	오믈렛	o-meul-let
boiled (e.g., ~ beef)	삶은	sal-meun
smoked (adj)	훈제된	hun-je-doen
fried (adj)	튀긴	twi-gin
dried (adj)	말린	mal-lin
frozen (adj)	얼린	eol-lin
pickled (adj)	초절인	cho-jeo-rin
sweet (sugary)	단	dan
salty (adj)	짠	jjan
cold (adj)	차가운	cha-ga-un
hot (adj)	뜨거운	tteu-geo-un
bitter (adj)	쓴	sseun
tasty (adj)	맛있는	man-nin-neun
to cook in boiling water	삶다	sam-da

to cook (dinner)	요리하다	yo-ri-ha-da
to fry (vt)	부치다	bu-chi-da
to heat up (food)	데우다	de-u-da

to salt (vt)	소금을 넣다	so-geu-meul leo-ta
to pepper (vt)	후추를 넣다	hu-chu-reul leo-ta
to grate (vt)	강판에 갈다	gang-pa-ne gal-da
peel (n)	껍질	kkeop-jil
to peel (vt)	껍질 벗기다	kkeop-jil beot-gi-da

41. Spices

salt	소금	so-geum
salty (adj)	짜	jja
to salt (vt)	소금을 넣다	so-geu-meul leo-ta

black pepper	후추	hu-chu
red pepper (milled ~)	고춧가루	go-chut-ga-ru
mustard	겨자	gyeo-ja
horseradish	고추냉이	go-chu-naeng-i

condiment	양념	yang-nyeom
spice	향료	hyang-nyo
sauce	소스	so-seu
vinegar	식초	sik-cho

anise	아니스	a-ni-seu
basil	바질	ba-jil
cloves	정향	jeong-hyang
ginger	생강	saeng-gang
coriander	고수	go-su
cinnamon	계피	gye-pi

sesame	깨	kkae
bay leaf	월계수잎	wol-gye-su-ip
paprika	파프리카	pa-peu-ri-ka
caraway	캐러웨이	kae-reo-we-i
saffron	사프란	sa-peu-ran

42. Meals

| food | 음식 | eum-sik |
| to eat (vi, vt) | 먹다 | meok-da |

breakfast	아침식사	a-chim-sik-sa
to have breakfast	아침을 먹다	a-chi-meul meok-da
lunch	점심식사	jeom-sim-sik-sa
to have lunch	점심을 먹다	jeom-si-meul meok-da

dinner	저녁식사	jeo-nyeok-sik-sa
to have dinner	저녁을 먹다	jeo-nyeo-geul meok-da
appetite	식욕	si-gyok
Enjoy your meal!	맛있게 드십시오!	man-nit-ge deu-sip-si-o!
to open (~ a bottle)	열다	yeol-da
to spill (liquid)	엎지르다	eop-ji-reu-da
to spill out (vi)	쏟아지다	sso-da-ji-da
to boil (vi)	끓다	kkeul-ta
to boil (vt)	끓이다	kkeu-ri-da
boiled (~ water)	끓인	kkeu-rin
to chill, cool down (vt)	식히다	sik-i-da
to chill (vi)	식다	sik-da
taste, flavor	맛	mat
aftertaste	뒷 맛	dwit mat
to slim down (lose weight)	살을 빼다	sa-reul ppae-da
diet	다이어트	da-i-eo-teu
vitamin	비타민	bi-ta-min
calorie	칼로리	kal-lo-ri
vegetarian (n)	채식주의자	chae-sik-ju-ui-ja
vegetarian (adj)	채식주의의	chae-sik-ju-ui-ui
fats (nutrient)	지방	ji-bang
proteins	단백질	dan-baek-jil
carbohydrates	탄수화물	tan-su-hwa-mul
slice (of lemon, ham)	조각	jo-gak
piece (of cake, pie)	조각	jo-gak
crumb (of bread, cake, etc.)	부스러기	bu-seu-reo-gi

43. Table setting

spoon	숟가락	sut-ga-rak
knife	나이프	na-i-peu
fork	포크	po-keu
cup (e.g., coffee ~)	컵	keop
plate (dinner ~)	접시	jeop-si
saucer	받침 접시	bat-chim jeop-si
napkin (on table)	냅킨	naep-kin
toothpick	이쑤시개	i-ssu-si-gae

44. Restaurant

restaurant	레스토랑	re-seu-to-rang
coffee house	커피숍	keo-pi-syop

| pub, bar | 바 | ba |
| tearoom | 카페, 티룸 | ka-pe, ti-rum |

waiter	웨이터	we-i-teo
waitress	웨이트리스	we-i-teu-ri-seu
bartender	바텐더	ba-ten-deo

menu	메뉴판	me-nyu-pan
wine list	와인 메뉴	wa-in me-nyu
to book a table	테이블 예약을 하다	te-i-beul rye-ya-geul ha-da

course, dish	요리, 코스	yo-ri, ko-seu
to order (meal)	주문하다	ju-mun-ha-da
to make an order	주문을 하다	ju-mu-neul ha-da

aperitif	아페리티프	a-pe-ri-ti-peu
appetizer	애피타이저	ae-pi-ta-i-jeo
dessert	디저트	di-jeo-teu

check	계산서	gye-san-seo
to pay the check	계산하다	gye-san-ha-da
to give change	거스름돈을 주다	geo-seu-reum-do-neul ju-da

| tip | 팁 | tip |

Family, relatives and friends

45. Personal information. Forms

name (first name)	이름	i-reum
surname (last name)	성	seong
date of birth	생년월일	saeng-nyeon-wo-ril
place of birth	탄생지	tan-saeng-ji
nationality	국적	guk-jeok
place of residence	거소	geo-so
country	나라	na-ra
profession (occupation)	직업	ji-geop
gender, sex	성별	seong-byeol
height	키	ki
weight	몸무게	mom-mu-ge

46. Family members. Relatives

mother	어머니	eo-meo-ni
father	아버지	a-beo-ji
son	아들	a-deul
daughter	딸	ttal
younger daughter	작은딸	ja-geun-ttal
younger son	작은아들	ja-geun-a-deul
eldest daughter	맏딸	mat-ttal
eldest son	맏아들	ma-da-deul
brother	형제	hyeong-je
sister	자매	ja-mae
cousin (masc.)	사촌 형제	sa-chon hyeong-je
cousin (fem.)	사촌 자매	sa-chon ja-mae
mom, mommy	엄마	eom-ma
dad, daddy	아빠	a-ppa
parents	부모	bu-mo
child	아이, 아동	a-i, a-dong
children	아이들	a-i-deul
grandmother	할머니	hal-meo-ni
grandfather	할아버지	ha-ra-beo-ji
grandson	손자	son-ja

granddaughter	손녀	son-nyeo
grandchildren	손자들	son-ja-deul
uncle	삼촌	sam-chon
nephew	조카	jo-ka
niece	조카딸	jo-ka-ttal
mother-in-law (wife's mother)	장모	jang-mo
father-in-law (husband's father)	시아버지	si-a-beo-ji
son-in-law (daughter's husband)	사위	sa-wi
stepmother	계모	gye-mo
stepfather	계부	gye-bu
infant	영아	yeong-a
baby (infant)	아기	a-gi
little boy, kid	꼬마	kko-ma
wife	아내	a-nae
husband	남편	nam-pyeon
spouse (husband)	배우자	bae-u-ja
spouse (wife)	배우자	bae-u-ja
married (masc.)	결혼한	gyeol-hon-han
married (fem.)	결혼한	gyeol-hon-han
single (unmarried)	미혼의	mi-hon-ui
bachelor	미혼 남자	mi-hon nam-ja
divorced (masc.)	이혼한	i-hon-han
widow	과부	gwa-bu
widower	홀아비	ho-ra-bi
relative	친척	chin-cheok
close relative	가까운 친척	ga-kka-un chin-cheok
distant relative	먼 친척	meon chin-cheok
relatives	친척들	chin-cheok-deul
orphan (boy or girl)	고아	go-a
guardian (of a minor)	후견인	hu-gyeon-in
to adopt (a boy)	입양하다	i-byang-ha-da
to adopt (a girl)	입양하다	i-byang-ha-da

Medicine

47. Diseases

sickness	병	byeong
to be sick	눕다	nup-da
health	건강	geon-gang
runny nose (coryza)	비염	bi-yeom
tonsillitis	편도염	pyeon-do-yeom
cold (illness)	감기	gam-gi
to catch a cold	감기에 걸리다	gam-gi-e geol-li-da
bronchitis	기관지염	gi-gwan-ji-yeom
pneumonia	폐렴	pye-ryeom
flu, influenza	독감	dok-gam
nearsighted (adj)	근시의	geun-si-ui
farsighted (adj)	원시의	won-si-ui
strabismus (crossed eyes)	사시	sa-si
cross-eyed (adj)	사시인	sa-si-in
cataract	백내장	baeng-nae-jang
glaucoma	녹내장	nong-nae-jang
stroke	뇌졸중	noe-jol-jung
heart attack	심장마비	sim-jang-ma-bi
myocardial infarction	심근경색증	sim-geun-gyeong-saek-jeung
paralysis	마비	ma-bi
to paralyze (vt)	마비되다	ma-bi-doe-da
allergy	알레르기	al-le-reu-gi
asthma	천식	cheon-sik
diabetes	당뇨병	dang-nyo-byeong
toothache	치통, 이앓이	chi-tong, i-a-ri
caries	충치	chung-chi
diarrhea	설사	seol-sa
constipation	변비증	byeon-bi-jeung
stomach upset	배탈	bae-tal
food poisoning	식중독	sik-jung-dok
to get food poisoning	식중독에 걸리다	sik-jung-do-ge geol-li-da
arthritis	관절염	gwan-jeo-ryeom
rickets	구루병	gu-ru-byeong

rheumatism	류머티즘	ryu-meo-ti-jeum
gastritis	위염	wi-yeom
appendicitis	맹장염	maeng-jang-yeom
cholecystitis	담낭염	dam-nang-yeom
ulcer	궤양	gwe-yang

measles	홍역	hong-yeok
rubella (German measles)	풍진	pung-jin
jaundice	황달	hwang-dal
hepatitis	간염	gan-nyeom

schizophrenia	정신 분열증	jeong-sin bu-nyeol-jeung
rabies (hydrophobia)	광견병	gwang-gyeon-byeong
neurosis	신경증	sin-gyeong-jeung
concussion	뇌진탕	noe-jin-tang

cancer	암	am
sclerosis	경화증	gyeong-hwa-jeung
multiple sclerosis	다발성 경화증	da-bal-seong gyeong-hwa-jeung

alcoholism	알코올 중독	al-ko-ol jung-dok
alcoholic (n)	알코올 중독자	al-ko-ol jung-dok-ja
syphilis	매독	mae-dok
AIDS	에이즈	e-i-jeu

tumor	종양	jong-yang
malignant (adj)	악성의	ak-seong-ui
benign (adj)	양성의	yang-seong-ui

fever	열병	yeol-byeong
malaria	말라리아	mal-la-ri-a
gangrene	괴저	goe-jeo
seasickness	뱃멀미	baen-meol-mi
epilepsy	간질	gan-jil

epidemic	유행병	yu-haeng-byeong
typhus	발진티푸스	bal-jin-ti-pu-seu
tuberculosis	결핵	gyeol-haek
cholera	콜레라	kol-le-ra
plague (bubonic ~)	페스트	pe-seu-teu

48. Symptoms. Treatments. Part 1

symptom	증상	jeung-sang
temperature	체온	che-on
high temperature (fever)	열	yeol
pulse	맥박	maek-bak
dizziness (vertigo)	현기증	hyeon-gi-jeung
hot (adj)	뜨거운	tteu-geo-un

shivering	전율	jeo-nyul
pale (e.g., ~ face)	창백한	chang-baek-an
cough	기침	gi-chim
to cough (vi)	기침을 하다	gi-chi-meul ha-da
to sneeze (vi)	재채기하다	jae-chae-gi-ha-da
faint	실신	sil-sin
to faint (vi)	실신하다	sil-sin-ha-da
bruise (hématome)	멍	meong
bump (lump)	혹	hok
to bang (bump)	부딪치다	bu-dit-chi-da
contusion (bruise)	타박상	ta-bak-sang
to get a bruise	타박상을 입다	ta-bak-sang-eul rip-da
to limp (vi)	절다	jeol-da
dislocation	탈구	tal-gu
to dislocate (vt)	탈구하다	tal-gu-ha-da
fracture	골절	gol-jeol
to have a fracture	골절하다	gol-jeol-ha-da
cut (e.g., paper ~)	베인	be-in
to cut oneself	베다	jeol-chang-eul rip-da
bleeding	출혈	chul-hyeol
burn (injury)	화상	hwa-sang
to get burned	데다	de-da
to prick (vt)	찌르다	jji-reu-da
to prick oneself	찔리다	jjil-li-da
to injure (vt)	다치다	da-chi-da
injury	부상	bu-sang
wound	부상	bu-sang
trauma	정신적 외상	jeong-sin-jeok goe-sang
to be delirious	망상을 겪다	mang-sang-eul gyeok-da
to stutter (vi)	말을 더듬다	ma-reul deo-deum-da
sunstroke	일사병	il-sa-byeong

49. Symptoms. Treatments. Part 2

pain, ache	통증	tong-jeung
splinter (in foot, etc.)	가시	ga-si
sweat (perspiration)	땀	ttam
to sweat (perspire)	땀이 나다	ttam-i na-da
vomiting	구토	gu-to
convulsions	경련	gyeong-nyeon
pregnant (adj)	임신한	im-sin-han
to be born	태어나다	tae-eo-na-da

delivery, labor	출산	chul-san
to deliver (~ a baby)	낳다	na-ta
abortion	낙태	nak-tae
breathing, respiration	호흡	ho-heup
in-breath (inhalation)	들숨	deul-sum
out-breath (exhalation)	날숨	nal-sum
to exhale (breathe out)	내쉬다	nae-swi-da
to inhale (vi)	들이쉬다	deu-ri-swi-da
disabled person	장애인	jang-ae-in
cripple	병신	byeong-sin
drug addict	마약 중독자	ma-yak jung-dok-ja
deaf (adj)	귀가 먼	gwi-ga meon
mute (adj)	벙어리인	beong-eo-ri-in
deaf mute (adj)	농아인	nong-a-in
mad, insane (adj)	미친	mi-chin
madman (demented person)	광인	gwang-in
madwoman	광인	gwang-in
to go insane	미치다	mi-chi-da
gene	유전자	yu-jeon-ja
immunity	면역성	myeo-nyeok-seong
hereditary (adj)	유전의	yu-jeon-ui
congenital (adj)	선천적인	seon-cheon-jeo-gin
virus	바이러스	ba-i-reo-seu
microbe	미생물	mi-saeng-mul
bacterium	세균	se-gyun
infection	감염	gam-nyeom

50. Symptoms. Treatments. Part 3

hospital	병원	byeong-won
patient	환자	hwan-ja
diagnosis	진단	jin-dan
cure	치료	chi-ryo
to get treatment	치료를 받다	chi-ryo-reul bat-da
to treat (~ a patient)	치료하다	chi-ryo-ha-da
to nurse (look after)	간호하다	gan-ho-ha-da
care (nursing ~)	간호	gan-ho
operation, surgery	수술	su-sul
to bandage (head, limb)	붕대를 감다	bung-dae-reul gam-da
bandaging	붕대	bung-dae
vaccination	예방주사	ye-bang-ju-sa

to vaccinate (vt)	접종하다	jeop-jong-ha-da
injection, shot	주사	ju-sa
to give an injection	주사하다	ju-sa-ha-da
amputation	절단	jeol-dan
to amputate (vt)	절단하다	jeol-dan-ha-da
coma	혼수 상태	hon-su sang-tae
to be in a coma	혼수 상태에 있다	hon-su sang-tae-e it-da
intensive care	집중 치료	jip-jung chi-ryo
to recover (~ from flu)	회복하다	hoe-bok-a-da
condition (patient's ~)	상태	sang-tae
consciousness	의식	ui-sik
memory (faculty)	기억	gi-eok
to pull out (tooth)	빼다	ppae-da
filling	충전물	chung-jeon-mul
to fill (a tooth)	때우다	ttae-u-da
hypnosis	최면	choe-myeon
to hypnotize (vt)	최면을 걸다	choe-myeo-neul geol-da

51. Doctors

doctor	의사	ui-sa
nurse	간호사	gan-ho-sa
personal doctor	개인 의사	gae-in ui-sa
dentist	치과 의사	chi-gwa ui-sa
eye doctor	안과 의사	an-gwa ui-sa
internist	내과 의사	nae-gwa ui-sa
surgeon	외과 의사	oe-gwa ui-sa
psychiatrist	정신과 의사	jeong-sin-gwa ui-sa
pediatrician	소아과 의사	so-a-gwa ui-sa
psychologist	심리학자	sim-ni-hak-ja
gynecologist	부인과 의사	bu-in-gwa ui-sa
cardiologist	심장병 전문의	sim-jang-byeong jeon-mun-ui

52. Medicine. Drugs. Accessories

medicine, drug	약	yak
remedy	약제	yak-je
prescription	처방	cheo-bang
tablet, pill	정제	jeong-je
ointment	연고	yeon-go

ampule	앰풀	aem-pul
mixture	혼합물	hon-ham-mul
syrup	물약	mul-lyak
pill	알약	a-ryak
powder	가루약	ga-ru-yak
gauze bandage	거즈 붕대	geo-jeu bung-dae
cotton wool	솜	som
iodine	요오드	yo-o-deu
Band-Aid	반창고	ban-chang-go
eyedropper	점안기	jeom-an-gi
thermometer	체온계	che-on-gye
syringe	주사기	ju-sa-gi
wheelchair	휠체어	hwil-che-eo
crutches	목발	mok-bal
painkiller	진통제	jin-tong-je
laxative	완하제	wan-ha-je
spirits (ethanol)	알코올	al-ko-ol
medicinal herbs	약초	yak-cho
herbal (~ tea)	약초의	yak-cho-ui

HUMAN HABITAT

City

53. City. Life in the city

city, town	도시	do-si
capital city	수도	su-do
village	마을	ma-eul
city map	도시 지도	do-si ji-do
downtown	시내	si-nae
suburb	근교	geun-gyo
suburban (adj)	근교의	geun-gyo-ui
environs (suburbs)	주변	ju-byeon
city block	한 구획	han gu-hoek
residential block (area)	동	dong
traffic	교통	gyo-tong
traffic lights	신호등	sin-ho-deung
public transportation	대중교통	dae-jung-gyo-tong
intersection	교차로	gyo-cha-ro
crosswalk	횡단 보도	hoeng-dan bo-do
pedestrian underpass	지하 보도	ji-ha bo-do
to cross (~ the street)	건너가다	geon-neo-ga-da
pedestrian	보행자	bo-haeng-ja
sidewalk	인도	in-do
bridge	다리	da-ri
embankment (river walk)	강변로	gang-byeon-no
allée (garden walkway)	길	gil
park	공원	gong-won
boulevard	대로	dae-ro
square	광장	gwang-jang
avenue (wide street)	가로	ga-ro
street	거리	geo-ri
side street	골목	gol-mok
dead end	막다른길	mak-da-reun-gil
house	집	jip
building	빌딩	bil-ding
skyscraper	고층 건물	go-cheung geon-mul

facade	전면	jeon-myeon
roof	지붕	ji-bung
window	창문	chang-mun
arch	아치	a-chi
column	기둥	gi-dung
corner	모퉁이	mo-tung-i

store window	쇼윈도우	syo-win-do-u
signboard (store sign, etc.)	간판	gan-pan
poster	포스터	po-seu-teo
advertising poster	광고 포스터	gwang-go po-seu-teo
billboard	광고판	gwang-go-pan

garbage, trash	쓰레기	sseu-re-gi
trashcan (public ~)	쓰레기통	sseu-re-gi-tong
garbage dump	쓰레기장	sseu-re-gi-jang

phone booth	공중 전화	gong-jung jeon-hwa
lamppost	가로등	ga-ro-deung
bench (park ~)	벤치	ben-chi

police officer	경찰관	gyeong-chal-gwan
police	경찰	gyeong-chal
beggar	거지	geo-ji
homeless (n)	노숙자	no-suk-ja

54. Urban institutions

store	가게, 상점	ga-ge, sang-jeom
drugstore, pharmacy	약국	yak-guk
eyeglass store	안경 가게	an-gyeong ga-ge
shopping mall	쇼핑몰	syo-ping-mol
supermarket	슈퍼마켓	syu-peo-ma-ket

bakery	빵집	ppang-jip
baker	제빵사	je-ppang-sa
pastry shop	제과점	je-gwa-jeom
grocery store	식료품점	sing-nyo-pum-jeom
butcher shop	정육점	jeong-yuk-jeom

| produce store | 야채 가게 | ya-chae ga-ge |
| market | 시장 | si-jang |

coffee house	커피숍	keo-pi-syop
restaurant	레스토랑	re-seu-to-rang
pub, bar	바	ba
pizzeria	피자 가게	pi-ja ga-ge

| hair salon | 미장원 | mi-jang-won |
| post office | 우체국 | u-che-guk |

| dry cleaners | 드라이 클리닝 | deu-ra-i keul-li-ning |
| photo studio | 사진관 | sa-jin-gwan |

shoe store	신발 가게	sin-bal ga-ge
bookstore	서점	seo-jeom
sporting goods store	스포츠용품 매장	seu-po-cheu-yong-pum mae-jang

clothes repair shop	옷 수선 가게	ot su-seon ga-ge
formal wear rental	의류 임대	ui-ryu im-dae
video rental store	비디오 대여	bi-di-o dae-yeo

circus	서커스	seo-keo-seu
zoo	동물원	dong-mu-rwon
movie theater	영화관	yeong-hwa-gwan
museum	박물관	bang-mul-gwan
library	도서관	do-seo-gwan

| theater | 극장 | geuk-jang |
| opera (opera house) | 오페라극장 | o-pe-ra-geuk-jang |

| nightclub | 나이트 클럽 | na-i-teu keul-leop |
| casino | 카지노 | ka-ji-no |

mosque	모스크	mo-seu-keu
synagogue	유대교 회당	yu-dae-gyo hoe-dang
cathedral	대성당	dae-seong-dang

| temple | 사원, 신전 | sa-won, sin-jeon |
| church | 교회 | gyo-hoe |

college	단과대학	dan-gwa-dae-hak
university	대학교	dae-hak-gyo
school	학교	hak-gyo

| prefecture | 도, 현 | do, hyeon |
| city hall | 시청 | si-cheong |

| hotel | 호텔 | ho-tel |
| bank | 은행 | eun-haeng |

| embassy | 대사관 | dae-sa-gwan |
| travel agency | 여행사 | yeo-haeng-sa |

| information office | 안내소 | an-nae-so |
| currency exchange | 환전소 | hwan-jeon-so |

| subway | 지하철 | ji-ha-cheol |
| hospital | 병원 | byeong-won |

| gas station | 주유소 | ju-yu-so |
| parking lot | 주차장 | ju-cha-jang |

55. Signs

signboard (store sign, etc.)	간판	gan-pan
notice (door sign, etc.)	안내문	an-nae-mun
poster	포스터	po-seu-teo
direction sign	방향표시	bang-hyang-pyo-si
arrow (sign)	화살표	hwa-sal-pyo
caution	경고	gyeong-go
warning sign	경고판	gyeong-go-pan
to warn (vt)	경고하다	gyeong-go-ha-da
rest day (weekly ~)	휴일	hyu-il
timetable (schedule)	시간표	si-gan-pyo
opening hours	영업 시간	yeong-eop si-gan
WELCOME!	어서 오세요!	eo-seo o-se-yo!
ENTRANCE	입구	ip-gu
EXIT	출구	chul-gu
PUSH	미세요	mi-se-yo
PULL	당기세요	dang-gi-se-yo
OPEN	열림	yeol-lim
CLOSED	닫힘	da-chim
WOMEN	여성전용	yeo-seong-jeo-nyong
MEN	남성	nam-seong-jeo-nyong
DISCOUNTS	할인	ha-rin
SALE	세일	se-il
NEW!	신상품	sin-sang-pum
FREE	공짜	gong-jja
ATTENTION!	주의!	ju-ui!
NO VACANCIES	빈 방 없음	bin bang eop-seum
RESERVED	예약석	ye-yak-seok
ADMINISTRATION	관리부	gwal-li-bu
STAFF ONLY	직원 전용	ji-gwon jeo-nyong
BEWARE OF THE DOG!	개조심	gae-jo-sim
NO SMOKING	금연	geu-myeon
DO NOT TOUCH!	손 대지 마시오!	son dae-ji ma-si-o!
DANGEROUS	위험	wi-heom
DANGER	위험	wi-heom
HIGH VOLTAGE	고전압	go-jeon-ap
NO SWIMMING!	수영 금지	su-yeong geum-ji
OUT OF ORDER	수리중	su-ri-jung
FLAMMABLE	가연성 물자	ga-yeon-seong mul-ja
FORBIDDEN	금지	geum-ji

| NO TRESPASSING! | 출입 금지 | chu-rip geum-ji |
| WET PAINT | 칠 주의 | chil ju-ui |

56. Urban transportation

bus	버스	beo-seu
streetcar	전차	jeon-cha
trolley bus	트롤리 버스	teu-rol-li beo-seu
route (of bus, etc.)	노선	no-seon
number (e.g., bus ~)	번호	beon-ho

to go by ...	… 타고 가다	… ta-go ga-da
to get on (~ the bus)	타다	ta-da
to get off ...	… 에서 내리다	… e-seo nae-ri-da

stop (e.g., bus ~)	정류장	jeong-nyu-jang
next stop	다음 정류장	da-eum jeong-nyu-jang
terminus	종점	jong-jeom
schedule	시간표	si-gan-pyo
to wait (vt)	기다리다	gi-da-ri-da

ticket	표	pyo
fare	요금	yo-geum
cashier (ticket seller)	계산원	gye-san-won
ticket inspection	검표	geom-pyo
ticket inspector	검표원	geom-pyo-won

to be late (for ...)	… 시간에 늦다	… si-gan-e neut-da
to miss (~ the train, etc.)	놓치다	no-chi-da
to be in a hurry	서두르다	seo-du-reu-da

taxi, cab	택시	taek-si
taxi driver	택시 운전 기사	taek-si un-jeon gi-sa
by taxi	택시로	taek-si-ro
taxi stand	택시 정류장	taek-si jeong-nyu-jang
to call a taxi	택시를 부르다	taek-si-reul bu-reu-da
to take a taxi	택시를 타다	taek-si-reul ta-da

traffic	교통	gyo-tong
traffic jam	교통 체증	gyo-tong che-jeung
rush hour	러시 아워	reo-si a-wo
to park (vi)	주차하다	ju-cha-ha-da
to park (vt)	주차하다	ju-cha-ha-da
parking lot	주차장	ju-cha-jang

subway	지하철	ji-ha-cheol
station	역	yeok
to take the subway	지하철을 타다	ji-ha-cheo-reul ta-da
train	기차	gi-cha
train station	기차역	gi-cha-yeok

57. Sightseeing

monument	기념비	gi-nyeom-bi
fortress	요새	yo-sae
palace	궁전	gung-jeon
castle	성	seong
tower	탑	tap
mausoleum	영묘	yeong-myo
architecture	건축	geon-chuk
medieval (adj)	중세의	jung-se-ui
ancient (adj)	고대의	go-dae-ui
national (adj)	국가의	guk-ga-ui
famous (monument, etc.)	유명한	yu-myeong-han
tourist	관광객	gwan-gwang-gaek
guide (person)	가이드	ga-i-deu
excursion, sightseeing tour	견학, 관광	gyeon-hak, gwan-gwang
to show (vt)	보여주다	bo-yeo-ju-da
to tell (vt)	이야기하다	i-ya-gi-ha-da
to find (vt)	찾다	chat-da
to get lost (lose one's way)	길을 잃다	gi-reul ril-ta
map (e.g., subway ~)	노선도	no-seon-do
map (e.g., city ~)	지도	ji-do
souvenir, gift	기념품	gi-nyeom-pum
gift shop	기념품 가게	gi-nyeom-pum ga-ge
to take pictures	사진을 찍다	sa-ji-neul jjik-da
to have one's picture taken	사진을 찍다	sa-ji-neul jjik-da

58. Shopping

to buy (purchase)	사다	sa-da
purchase	구매	gu-mae
to go shopping	쇼핑하다	syo-ping-ha-da
shopping	쇼핑	syo-ping
to be open (ab. store)	열리다	yeol-li-da
to be closed	닫다	dat-da
footwear, shoes	신발	sin-bal
clothes, clothing	옷	ot
cosmetics	화장품	hwa-jang-pum
food products	식품	sik-pum
gift, present	선물	seon-mul
salesman	판매원	pan-mae-won
saleswoman	여판매원	yeo-pan-mae-won

check out, cash desk	계산대	gye-san-dae
mirror	거울	geo-ul
counter (store ~)	계산대	gye-san-dae
fitting room	탈의실	ta-rui-sil
to try on	입어보다	i-beo-bo-da
to fit (ab. dress, etc.)	어울리다	eo-ul-li-da
to like (I like ...)	좋아하다	jo-a-ha-da
price	가격	ga-gyeok
price tag	가격표	ga-gyeok-pyo
to cost (vt)	값이 … 이다	gap-si ... i-da
How much?	얼마?	eol-ma?
discount	할인	ha-rin
inexpensive (adj)	비싸지 않은	bi-ssa-ji a-neun
cheap (adj)	싼	ssan
expensive (adj)	비싼	bi-ssan
It's expensive	비쌉니다	bi-ssam-ni-da
rental (n)	임대	im-dae
to rent (~ a tuxedo)	빌리다	bil-li-da
credit (trade credit)	신용	si-nyong
on credit (adv)	신용으로	si-nyong-eu-ro

59. Money

money	돈	don
currency exchange	환전	hwan-jeon
exchange rate	환율	hwa-nyul
ATM	현금 자동 지급기	hyeon-geum ja-dong ji-geup-gi
coin	동전	dong-jeon
dollar	달러	dal-leo
euro	유로	yu-ro
lira	리라	ri-ra
Deutschmark	마르크	ma-reu-keu
franc	프랑	peu-rang
pound sterling	파운드	pa-un-deu
yen	엔	en
debt	빚	bit
debtor	채무자	chae-mu-ja
to lend (money)	빌려주다	bil-lyeo-ju-da
to borrow (vi, vt)	빌리다	bil-li-da
bank	은행	eun-haeng
account	계좌	gye-jwa

| to deposit into the account | 계좌에 입금하다 | ip-geum-ha-da |
| to withdraw (vt) | 출금하다 | chul-geum-ha-da |

credit card	신용 카드	si-nyong ka-deu
cash	현금	hyeon-geum
check	수표	su-pyo
to write a check	수표를 끊다	su-pyo-reul kkeun-ta
checkbook	수표책	su-pyo-chaek

wallet	지갑	ji-gap
change purse	동전지갑	dong-jeon-ji-gap
safe	금고	geum-go

heir	상속인	sang-so-gin
inheritance	유산	yu-san
fortune (wealth)	재산, 큰돈	jae-san, keun-don

lease	임대	im-dae
rent (money)	집세	jip-se
to rent (sth from sb)	임대하다	im-dae-ha-da

price	가격	ga-gyeok
cost	비용	bi-yong
sum	액수	aek-su

to spend (vt)	쓰다	sseu-da
expenses	출비를	chul-bi-reul
to economize (vi, vt)	절약하다	jeo-ryak-a-da
economical	경제적인	gyeong-je-jeo-gin

to pay (vi, vt)	지불하다	ji-bul-ha-da
payment	지불	ji-bul
change (give the ~)	거스름돈	geo-seu-reum-don

tax	세금	se-geum
fine	벌금	beol-geum
to fine (vt)	벌금을 부과하다	beol-geu-meul bu-gwa-ha-da

60. Post. Postal service

post office	우체국	u-che-guk
mail (letters, etc.)	우편물	u-pyeon-mul
mailman	우체부	u-che-bu
opening hours	영업 시간	yeong-eop si-gan

letter	편지	pyeon-ji
registered letter	등기 우편	deung-gi u-pyeon
postcard	엽서	yeop-seo
telegram	전보	jeon-bo

| package (parcel) | 소포 | so-po |
| money transfer | 송금 | song-geum |

to receive (vt)	받다	bat-da
to send (vt)	보내다	bo-nae-da
sending	발송	bal-song

address	주소	ju-so
ZIP code	우편 번호	u-pyeon beon-ho
sender	발송인	bal-song-in
receiver	수신인	su-sin-in

| name (first name) | 이름 | i-reum |
| surname (last name) | 성 | seong |

postage rate	요금	yo-geum
standard (adj)	일반의	il-ba-nui
economical (adj)	경제적인	gyeong-je-jeo-gin

weight	무게	mu-ge
to weigh (~ letters)	무게를 달다	mu-ge-reul dal-da
envelope	봉투	bong-tu
postage stamp	우표	u-pyo

Dwelling. House. Home

61. House. Electricity

electricity	전기	jeon-gi
light bulb	전구	jeon-gu
switch	스위치	seu-wi-chi
fuse (plug fuse)	퓨즈	pyu-jeu
cable, wire (electric ~)	전선	jeon-seon
wiring	배선	bae-seon
electricity meter	전기 계량기	jeon-gi gye-ryang-gi
readings	판독값	pan-dok-gap

62. Villa. Mansion

country house	시외 주택	si-oe ju-taek
villa (seaside ~)	별장	byeol-jang
wing (~ of a building)	동	dong
garden	정원	jeong-won
park	공원	gong-won
tropical greenhouse	열대온실	yeol-dae-on-sil
to look after (garden, etc.)	… 을 맡다	… eul mat-da
swimming pool	수영장	su-yeong-jang
gym (home gym)	헬스장	hel-seu-jang
tennis court	테니스장	te-ni-seu-jang
home theater (room)	홈씨어터	hom-ssi-eo-teo
garage	차고	cha-go
private property	개인 소유물	gae-in so-yu-mul
private land	사유 토지	sa-yu to-ji
warning (caution)	경고	gyeong-go
warning sign	경고판	gyeong-go-pan
security	보안	bo-an
security guard	보안요원	bo-a-nyo-won
burglar alarm	도난 경보기	do-nan gyeong-bo-gi

63. Apartment

apartment	아파트	a-pa-teu
room	방	bang
bedroom	침실	chim-sil
dining room	식당	sik-dang
living room	거실	geo-sil
study (home office)	서재	seo-jae
entry room	곁방	gyeot-bang
bathroom (room with a bath or shower)	욕실	yok-sil
half bath	화장실	hwa-jang-sil
ceiling	천장	cheon-jang
floor	마루	ma-ru
corner	구석	gu-seok

64. Furniture. Interior

furniture	가구	ga-gu
table	식탁, 테이블	sik-tak, te-i-beul
chair	의자	ui-ja
bed	침대	chim-dae
couch, sofa	소파	so-pa
armchair	안락 의자	al-lak gui-ja
bookcase	책장	chaek-jang
shelf	책꽂이	chaek-kko-ji
wardrobe	옷장	ot-jang
coat rack (wall-mounted ~)	옷걸이	ot-geo-ri
coat stand	스탠드옷걸이	seu-taen-deu-ot-geo-ri
bureau, dresser	서랍장	seo-rap-jang
coffee table	커피 테이블	keo-pi te-i-beul
mirror	거울	geo-ul
carpet	양탄자	yang-tan-ja
rug, small carpet	러그	reo-geu
fireplace	벽난로	byeong-nan-no
candle	초	cho
candlestick	촛대	chot-dae
drapes	커튼	keo-teun
wallpaper	벽지	byeok-ji
blinds (jalousie)	블라인드	beul-la-in-deu
table lamp	테이블 램프	deung

wall lamp (sconce)	벽등	byeok-deung
floor lamp	플로어 스탠드	peul-lo-eo seu-taen-deu
chandelier	샹들리에	syang-deul-li-e

leg (of chair, table)	다리	da-ri
armrest	팔걸이	pal-geo-ri
back (backrest)	등받이	deung-ba-ji
drawer	서랍	seo-rap

65. Bedding

bedclothes	침구	chim-gu
pillow	베개	be-gae
pillowcase	베갯잇	be-gaen-nit
duvet, comforter	이불	i-bul
sheet	시트	si-teu
bedspread	침대보	chim-dae-bo

66. Kitchen

kitchen	부엌	bu-eok
gas	가스	ga-seu
gas stove (range)	가스 레인지	ga-seu re-in-ji
electric stove	전기 레인지	jeon-gi re-in-ji
oven	오븐	o-beun
microwave oven	전자 레인지	jeon-ja re-in-ji

refrigerator	냉장고	naeng-jang-go
freezer	냉동고	naeng-dong-go
dishwasher	식기 세척기	sik-gi se-cheok-gi

meat grinder	고기 분쇄기	go-gi bun-swae-gi
juicer	과즙기	gwa-jeup-gi
toaster	토스터	to-seu-teo
mixer	믹서기	mik-seo-gi

coffee machine	커피 메이커	keo-pi me-i-keo
coffee pot	커피 주전자	keo-pi ju-jeon-ja
coffee grinder	커피 그라인더	keo-pi geu-ra-in-deo

kettle	주전자	ju-jeon-ja
teapot	티팟	ti-pat
lid	뚜껑	ttu-kkeong
tea strainer	차거름망	cha-geo-reum-mang

spoon	숟가락	sut-ga-rak
teaspoon	티스푼	ti-seu-pun
soup spoon	숟가락	sut-ga-rak

fork	포크	po-keu
knife	칼	kal
tableware (dishes)	식기	sik-gi
plate (dinner ~)	접시	jeop-si
saucer	받침 접시	bat-chim jeop-si
shot glass	소주잔	so-ju-jan
glass (tumbler)	유리잔	yu-ri-jan
cup	컵	keop
sugar bowl	설탕그릇	seol-tang-geu-reut
salt shaker	소금통	so-geum-tong
pepper shaker	후추통	hu-chu-tong
butter dish	버터 접시	beo-teo jeop-si
stock pot (soup pot)	냄비	naem-bi
frying pan (skillet)	프라이팬	peu-ra-i-paen
ladle	국자	guk-ja
colander	체	che
tray (serving ~)	쟁반	jaeng-ban
bottle	병	byeong
jar (glass)	유리병	yu-ri-byeong
can	캔, 깡통	kaen, kkang-tong
bottle opener	병따개	byeong-tta-gae
can opener	깡통 따개	kkang-tong tta-gae
corkscrew	코르크 마개 뽑이	ko-reu-keu ma-gae ppo-bi
filter	필터	pil-teo
to filter (vt)	여과하다	yeo-gwa-ha-da
trash, garbage (food waste, etc.)	쓰레기	sseu-re-gi
trash can (kitchen ~)	쓰레기통	sseu-re-gi-tong

67. Bathroom

bathroom	욕실	yok-sil
water	물	mul
faucet	수도꼭지	su-do-kkok-ji
hot water	온수	on-su
cold water	냉수	naeng-su
toothpaste	치약	chi-yak
to brush one's teeth	이를 닦다	i-reul dak-da
to shave (vi)	깎다	kkak-da
shaving foam	면도 크림	myeon-do keu-rim
razor	면도기	myeon-do-gi

to wash (one's hands, etc.)	씻다	ssit-da
to take a bath	목욕하다	mo-gyok-a-da
shower	샤워	sya-wo
to take a shower	샤워하다	sya-wo-ha-da
bathtub	욕조	yok-jo
toilet (toilet bowl)	변기	byeon-gi
sink (washbasin)	세면대	se-myeon-dae
soap	비누	bi-nu
soap dish	비누 그릇	bi-nu geu-reut
sponge	스펀지	seu-peon-ji
shampoo	샴푸	syam-pu
towel	수건	su-geon
bathrobe	목욕가운	mo-gyok-ga-un
laundry (process)	빨래	ppal-lae
washing machine	세탁기	se-tak-gi
to do the laundry	빨래하다	ppal-lae-ha-da
laundry detergent	가루세제	ga-ru-se-je

68. Household appliances

TV set	텔레비전	tel-le-bi-jeon
tape recorder	카세트 플레이어	ka-se-teu peul-le-i-eo
VCR (video recorder)	비디오테이프 녹화기	bi-di-o-te-i-peu nok-wa-gi
radio	라디오	ra-di-o
player (CD, MP3, etc.)	플레이어	peul-le-i-eo
video projector	프로젝터	peu-ro-jek-teo
home movie theater	홈씨어터	hom-ssi-eo-teo
DVD player	디비디 플레이어	di-bi-di peul-le-i-eo
amplifier	앰프	aem-peu
video game console	게임기	ge-im-gi
video camera	캠코더	kaem-ko-deo
camera (photo)	카메라	ka-me-ra
digital camera	디지털 카메라	di-ji-teol ka-me-ra
vacuum cleaner	진공 청소기	jin-gong cheong-so-gi
iron (e.g., steam ~)	다리미	da-ri-mi
ironing board	다림질 판	da-rim-jil pan
telephone	전화	jeon-hwa
cell phone	휴대폰	hyu-dae-pon
typewriter	타자기	ta-ja-gi
sewing machine	재봉틀	jae-bong-teul
microphone	마이크	ma-i-keu
headphones	헤드폰	he-deu-pon

remote control (TV)	원격 조종	won-gyeok jo-jong
CD, compact disc	씨디	ssi-di
cassette, tape	테이프	te-i-peu
vinyl record	레코드 판	re-ko-deu pan

HUMAN ACTIVITIES

Job. Business. Part 1

69. Office. Working in the office

office (company ~)	사무실	sa-mu-sil
office (of director, etc.)	사무실	sa-mu-sil
reception desk	접수처	jeop-su-cheo
secretary	비서	bi-seo
director	사장	sa-jang
manager	매니저	mae-ni-jeo
accountant	회계사	hoe-gye-sa
employee	직원	ji-gwon
furniture	가구	ga-gu
desk	책상	chaek-sang
desk chair	책상 의자	chaek-sang ui-ja
coat stand	스탠드옷걸이	seu-taen-deu-ot-geo-ri
computer	컴퓨터	keom-pyu-teo
printer	프린터	peu-rin-teo
fax machine	팩스기	paek-seu-gi
photocopier	복사기	bok-sa-gi
paper	종이	jong-i
office supplies	사무용품	sa-mu-yong-pum
mouse pad	마우스 패드	ma-u-seu pae-deu
sheet (of paper)	한 장	han jang
binder	바인더	ba-in-deo
catalog	카탈로그	ka-tal-lo-geu
phone directory	전화번호부	jeon-hwa-beon-ho-bu
documentation	문서	mun-seo
brochure (e.g., 12 pages ~)	브로셔	beu-ro-syeo
leaflet (promotional ~)	전단	jeon-dan
sample	샘플	saem-peul
training meeting	수련회를	su-ryeon-hoe-reul
meeting (of managers)	회의	hoe-ui
lunch time	점심시간	jeom-sim-si-gan
to make a copy	사본을 만들다	sa-bo-neul man-deul-da
to make multiple copies	복사하다	bok-sa-ha-da

| to receive a fax | 팩스를 받다 | paek-seu-reul bat-da |
| to send a fax | 팩스를 보내다 | paek-seu-reul bo-nae-da |

to call (by phone)	전화하다	jeon-hwa-ha-da
to answer (vt)	대답하다	dae-da-pa-da
to put through	연결해 주다	yeon-gyeol-hae ju-da

to arrange, to set up	마련하다	ma-ryeon-ha-da
to demonstrate (vt)	전시하다	jeon-si-ha-da
to be absent	결석하다	gyeol-seok-a-da
absence	결근	gyeol-geun

70. Business processes. Part 1

occupation	직업	ji-geop
firm	회사	hoe-sa
company	회사	hoe-sa
corporation	사단 법인	sa-dan beo-bin
enterprise	업체	eop-che
agency	에이전시	e-i-jeon-si

agreement (contract)	약정	yak-jeong
contract	계약	gye-yak
deal	거래	geo-rae
order (to place an ~)	주문	ju-mun
terms (of the contract)	조건	jo-geon

wholesale (adv)	도매로	do-mae-ro
wholesale (adj)	도매의	do-mae-ui
wholesale (n)	도매	do-mae
retail (adj)	소매의	so-mae-ui
retail (n)	소매	so-mae

competitor	경쟁자	gyeong-jaeng-ja
competition	경쟁	gyeong-jaeng
to compete (vi)	경쟁하다	gyeong-jaeng-ha-da

| partner (associate) | 파트너 | pa-teu-neo |
| partnership | 파트너십 | pa-teu-neo-sip |

crisis	위기	wi-gi
bankruptcy	파산	pa-san
to go bankrupt	파산하다	pa-san-ha-da
difficulty	어려움	eo-ryeo-um
problem	문제	mun-je
catastrophe	재난	jae-nan

economy	경기, 경제	gyeong-gi, gyeong-je
economic (~ growth)	경제의	gyeong-je-ui
economic recession	경기침체	gyeong-gi-chim-che

goal (aim)	목표	mok-pyo
task	임무	im-mu
to trade (vi)	거래하다	geo-rae-ha-da
network (distribution ~)	네트워크	ne-teu-wo-keu
inventory (stock)	재고	jae-go
range (assortment)	세트	se-teu
leader (leading company)	리더	ri-deo
large (~ company)	규모가 큰	gyu-mo-ga keun
monopoly	독점	dok-jeom
theory	이론	i-ron
practice	실천	sil-cheon
experience (in my ~)	경험	gyeong-heom
trend (tendency)	경향	gyeong-hyang
development	개발	gae-bal

71. Business processes. Part 2

profit (foregone ~)	수익, 이익	su-ik, i-ik
profitable (~ deal)	수익성이 있는	su-ik-seong-i in-neun
delegation (group)	대표단	dae-pyo-dan
salary	급여, 월급	geu-byeo, wol-geup
to correct (an error)	고치다	go-chi-da
business trip	출장	chul-jang
commission	수수료	su-su-ryo
to control (vt)	제어하다	je-eo-ha-da
conference	회의	hoe-ui
license	면허증	myeon-heo-jeung
reliable (~ partner)	믿을 만한	mi-deul man-han
initiative (undertaking)	시작	si-jak
norm (standard)	표준	pyo-jun
circumstance	상황	sang-hwang
duty (of employee)	의무	ui-mu
organization (company)	조직	jo-jik
organization (process)	준비	jun-bi
organized (adj)	조직된	jo-jik-doen
cancellation	취소	chwi-so
to cancel (call off)	취소하다	chwi-so-ha-da
report (official ~)	보고서	bo-go-seo
patent	특허	teuk-eo
to patent (obtain patent)	특허를 받다	teuk-eo-reul bat-da
to plan (vt)	계획하다	gye-hoek-a-da
bonus (money)	보너스	bo-neo-seu

professional (adj)	전문가의	jeon-mun-ga-ui
procedure	절차	jeol-cha
to examine (contract, etc.)	조사하다	jo-sa-ha-da
calculation	계산	gye-san
reputation	평판	pyeong-pan
risk	위험	wi-heom
to manage, to run	운영하다	u-nyeong-ha-da
information	정보	jeong-bo
property	소유	so-yu
union	연합	yeon-hap
life insurance	생명 보험	saeng-myeong bo-heom
to insure (vt)	보험에 들다	bo-heom-e deul-da
insurance	보험	bo-heom
auction (~ sale)	경매	gyeong-mae
to notify (inform)	통지하다	tong-ji-ha-da
management (process)	주관	ju-gwan
service (~ industry)	서비스	seo-bi-seu
forum	포럼	po-reom
to function (vi)	기능하다	gi-neung-ha-da
stage (phase)	단계	dan-gye
legal (~ services)	법률상의	beom-nyul-sang-ui
lawyer (legal advisor)	법률고문	beom-nyul-go-mun

72. Production. Works

plant	공장	gong-jang
factory	공장	gong-jang
workshop	작업장	ja-geop-jang
works, production site	현장	hyeon-jang
industry (manufacturing)	산업, 공업	san-eop, gong-eop
industrial (adj)	산업의	san-eo-bui
heavy industry	중공업	jung-gong-eop
light industry	경공업	gyeong-gong-eop
products	제품	je-pum
to produce (vt)	제조하다	je-jo-ha-da
raw materials	원재료	won-jae-ryo
foreman (construction ~)	작업반장	ja-geop-ban-jang
workers team (crew)	작업반	ja-geop-ban
worker	노동자	no-dong-ja
working day	근무일	geun-mu-il
pause (rest break)	휴식	hyu-sik

meeting	회의	hoe-ui
to discuss (vt)	의논하다	ui-non-ha-da
plan	계획	gye-hoek
to fulfill the plan	계획을 수행하다	gye-hoe-geul su-haeng-ha-da
rate of output	생산량	saeng-sal-lyang
quality	품질	pum-jil
control (checking)	관리	gwal-li
quality control	품질 관리	pum-jil gwal-li
workplace safety	산업안전	sa-neo-ban-jeon
discipline	규율	gyu-yul
violation (of safety rules, etc.)	위반	wi-ban
to violate (rules)	위반하다	wi-ban-ha-da
strike	파업	pa-eop
striker	파업자	pa-eop-ja
to be on strike	파업하다	pa-eo-pa-da
labor union	노동조합	no-dong-jo-hap
to invent (machine, etc.)	발명하다	bal-myeong-ha-da
invention	발명	bal-myeong
research	연구	yeon-gu
to improve (make better)	개선하다	gae-seon-ha-da
technology	기술	gi-sul
technical drawing	건축 도면	geon-chuk do-myeon
load, cargo	화물	hwa-mul
loader (person)	하역부	ha-yeok-bu
to load (vehicle, etc.)	싣다	sit-da
loading (process)	적재	jeok-jae
to unload (vi, vt)	짐을 부리다	ji-meul bu-ri-da
unloading	짐부리기	jim-bu-ri-gi
transportation	운송	un-song
transportation company	운송 회사	un-song hoe-sa
to transport (vt)	운송하다	un-song-ha-da
freight car	화차	hwa-cha
tank (e.g., oil ~)	탱크	taeng-keu
truck	트럭	teu-reok
machine tool	공작 기계	gong-jak gi-gye
mechanism	기계 장치	gi-gye jang-chi
industrial waste	산업폐기물	san-eop-pye-gi-mul
packing (process)	포장	po-jang
to pack (vt)	포장하다	po-jang-ha-da

73. Contract. Agreement

contract	계약	gye-yak
agreement	약정	yak-jeong
addendum	별첨	byeol-cheom
to sign a contract	계약에 서명하다	gye-ya-ge seo-myeong-ha-da
signature	서명	seo-myeong
to sign (vt)	서명하다	seo-myeong-ha-da
seal (stamp)	도장	do-jang
subject of contract	계약 내용	gye-yak nae-yong
clause	항	hang
parties (in contract)	양측	yang-cheuk
legal address	법인 주소	beo-bin ju-so
to violate the contract	계약을 위반하다	gye-ya-geul rwi-ban-ha-da
commitment (obligation)	의무	ui-mu
responsibility	책임	chae-gim
force majeure	불가항력	bul-ga-hang-nyeok
dispute	분쟁	bun-jaeng
penalties	제재	je-jae

74. Import & Export

import	수입	su-ip
importer	수입업자	su-i-beop-ja
to import (vt)	수입하다	su-i-pa-da
import (as adj.)	수입의	su-i-bui
exporter	수출업자	su-chu-reop-ja
to export (vi, vt)	수출하다	su-chul-ha-da
goods (merchandise)	상품	sang-pum
consignment, lot	탁송물	tak-song-mul
weight	무게	mu-ge
volume	부피	bu-pi
cubic meter	입방 미터	ip-bang mi-teo
manufacturer	생산자	saeng-san-ja
transportation company	운송 회사	un-song hoe-sa
container	컨테이너	keon-te-i-neo
border	국경	guk-gyeong
customs	세관	se-gwan
customs duty	관세	gwan-se
customs officer	세관원	se-gwan-won

| smuggling | 밀수입 | mil-su-ip |
| contraband (smuggled goods) | 밀수품 | mil-su-pum |

75. Finances

stock (share)	주식	ju-sik
bond (certificate)	채권	chae-gwon
promissory note	어음	eo-eum

| stock exchange | 증권거래소 | jeung-gwon-geo-rae-so |
| stock price | 주가 | ju-ga |

| to go down (become cheaper) | 내리다 | nae-ri-da |
| to go up (become more expensive) | 오르다 | o-reu-da |

controlling interest	지배 지분	ji-bae ji-bun
investment	투자	tu-ja
to invest (vt)	투자하다	tu-ja-ha-da

| percent | 퍼센트 | peo-sen-teu |
| interest (on investment) | 이자 | i-ja |

profit	수익, 이익	su-ik, i-ik
profitable (adj)	수익성이 있는	su-ik-seong-i in-neun
tax	세금	se-geum

currency (foreign ~)	통화	tong-hwa
national (adj)	국가의	guk-ga-ui
exchange (currency ~)	환전	hwan-jeon

| accountant | 회계사 | hoe-gye-sa |
| accounting | 회계 | hoe-gye |

bankruptcy	파산	pa-san
collapse, crash	붕괴	bung-goe
ruin	파산	pa-san
to be ruined (financially)	파산하다	pa-san-ha-da

| inflation | 인플레이션 | in-peul-le-i-syeon |
| devaluation | 평가절하 | pyeong-ga-jeol-ha |

capital	자본	ja-bon
income	소득	so-deuk
turnover	총매출액	chong-mae-chu-raek
resources	재원을	jae-wo-neul
monetary resources	재정 자원을	jae-jeong ja-wo-neul
to reduce (expenses)	줄이다	ju-ri-da

76. Marketing

marketing	마케팅	ma-ke-ting
market	시장	si-jang
market segment	시장 분야	si-jang bu-nya
product	제품	je-pum
goods (merchandise)	상품	sang-pum
trademark	트레이드마크	teu-re-i-deu-ma-keu
logotype	로고	ro-go
logo	로고	ro-go
demand	수요	su-yo
supply	공급	gong-geup
need	필요	pi-ryo
consumer	소비자	so-bi-ja
analysis	분석	bun-seok
to analyze (vt)	분석하다	bun-seok-a-da
positioning	포지셔닝	po-ji-syeo-ning
to position (vt)	포지셔닝하다	po-ji-syeo-ning-ha-da
price	가격	ga-gyeok
pricing policy	가격 정책	ga-gyeok jeong-chaek
price formation	가격 형성	ga-gyeok yeong-seong

77. Advertising

advertising	광고	gwang-go
to advertise (vt)	광고하다	gwang-go-ha-da
budget	예산	ye-san
ad, advertisement	광고	gwang-go
TV advertising	텔레비전 광고	tel-le-bi-jeon gwang-go
radio advertising	라디오 광고	ra-di-o gwang-go
outdoor advertising	옥외 광고	o-goe gwang-go
mass media	매체	mae-che
periodical (n)	정기 간행물	jeong-gi gan-haeng-mul
image (public appearance)	이미지	i-mi-ji
slogan	슬로건	seul-lo-geon
motto (maxim)	표어	pyo-eo
campaign	캠페인	kaem-pe-in
advertising campaign	광고 캠페인	gwang-go kaem-pe-in
target group	공략 대상	gong-nyak dae-sang
business card	명함	myeong-ham
leaflet (promotional ~)	전단	jeon-dan

brochure (e.g., 12 pages ~)	브로셔	beu-ro-syeo
pamphlet	팜플렛	pam-peul-let
newsletter	회보	hoe-bo
signboard (store sign, etc.)	간판	gan-pan
poster	포스터	po-seu-teo
billboard	광고판	gwang-go-pan

78. Banking

bank	은행	eun-haeng
branch (of bank, etc.)	지점	ji-jeom
bank clerk, consultant	행원	haeng-won
manager (director)	지배인	ji-bae-in
bank account	은행계좌	eun-haeng-gye-jwa
account number	계좌 번호	gye-jwa beon-ho
checking account	당좌	dang-jwa
savings account	보통 예금	bo-tong ye-geum
to open an account	계좌를 열다	gye-jwa-reul ryeol-da
to close the account	계좌를 해지하다	gye-jwa-reul hae-ji-ha-da
to deposit into the account	계좌에 입금하다	ip-geum-ha-da
to withdraw (vt)	출금하다	chul-geum-ha-da
deposit	저금	jeo-geum
to make a deposit	입금하다	ip-geum-ha-da
wire transfer	송금	song-geum
to wire, to transfer	송금하다	song-geum-ha-da
sum	액수	aek-su
How much?	얼마?	eol-ma?
signature	서명	seo-myeong
to sign (vt)	서명하다	seo-myeong-ha-da
credit card	신용 카드	si-nyong ka-deu
code (PIN code)	비밀번호	bi-mil-beon-ho
credit card number	신용 카드 번호	si-nyong ka-deu beon-ho
ATM	현금 자동 지급기	hyeon-geum ja-dong ji-geup-gi
check	수표	su-pyo
to write a check	수표를 끊다	su-pyo-reul kkeun-ta
checkbook	수표책	su-pyo-chaek
loan (bank ~)	대출	dae-chul
to apply for a loan	대출 신청하다	dae-chul sin-cheong-ha-da

to get a loan	대출을 받다	dae-chu-reul bat-da
to give a loan	대출하다	dae-chul-ha-da
guarantee	담보	dam-bo

79. Telephone. Phone conversation

telephone	전화	jeon-hwa
cell phone	휴대폰	hyu-dae-pon
answering machine	자동 응답기	ja-dong eung-dap-gi

| to call (by phone) | 전화하다 | jeon-hwa-ha-da |
| phone call | 통화 | tong-hwa |

to dial a number	번호로 걸다	beon-ho-ro geol-da
Hello!	여보세요!	yeo-bo-se-yo!
to ask (vt)	묻다	mut-da
to answer (vi, vt)	전화를 받다	jeon-hwa-reul bat-da

to hear (vt)	듣다	deut-da
well (adv)	잘	jal
not well (adv)	좋지 않은	jo-chi a-neun
noises (interference)	잡음	ja-beum

receiver	수화기	su-hwa-gi
to pick up (~ the phone)	전화를 받다	jeon-hwa-reul bat-da
to hang up (~ the phone)	전화를 끊다	jeon-hwa-reul kkeun-ta

busy (engaged)	통화 중인	tong-hwa jung-in
to ring (ab. phone)	울리다	ul-li-da
telephone book	전화 번호부	jeon-hwa beon-ho-bu

local (adj)	시내의	si-nae-ui
long distance (~ call)	장거리의	jang-geo-ri-ui
international (adj)	국제적인	guk-je-jeo-gin

80. Cell phone

cell phone	휴대폰	hyu-dae-pon
display	화면	hwa-myeon
button	버튼	beo-teun
SIM card	SIM 카드	SIM ka-deu

battery	건전지	geon-jeon-ji
to be dead (battery)	나가다	na-ga-da
charger	충전기	chung-jeon-gi

| menu | 메뉴 | me-nyu |
| settings | 설정 | seol-jeong |

| tune (melody) | 벨소리 | bel-so-ri |
| to select (vt) | 선택하다 | seon-taek-a-da |

calculator	계산기	gye-san-gi
voice mail	자동 응답기	ja-dong eung-dap-gi
alarm clock	알람 시계	al-lam si-gye
contacts	연락처	yeol-lak-cheo

| SMS (text message) | 문자 메시지 | mun-ja me-si-ji |
| subscriber | 가입자 | ga-ip-ja |

81. Stationery

| ballpoint pen | 볼펜 | bol-pen |
| fountain pen | 만년필 | man-nyeon-pil |

pencil	연필	yeon-pil
highlighter	형광펜	hyeong-gwang-pen
felt-tip pen	사인펜	sa-in-pen

| notepad | 공책 | gong-chaek |
| agenda (diary) | 수첩 | su-cheop |

ruler	자	ja
calculator	계산기	gye-san-gi
eraser	지우개	ji-u-gae
thumbtack	압정	ap-jeong
paper clip	클립	keul-lip

glue	접착제	jeop-chak-je
stapler	호치키스	ho-chi-ki-seu
hole punch	펀치	peon-chi
pencil sharpener	연필깎이	yeon-pil-kka-kki

82. Kinds of business

accounting services	회계 서비스	hoe-gye seo-bi-seu
advertising	광고	gwang-go
advertising agency	광고 회사	gwang-go hoe-sa
air-conditioners	에어컨	e-eo-keon
airline	항공사	hang-gong-sa

alcoholic beverages	주류	ju-ryu
antiques (antique dealers)	골동품	gol-dong-pum
art gallery (contemporary ~)	미술관	mi-sul-gwan
audit services	회계 감사	hoe-gye gam-sa
banking industry	금융업계	geu-myung-eop-gye

bar	바	ba
beauty parlor	미장원	mi-jang-won
bookstore	서점	seo-jeom
brewery	맥주 양조장	maek-ju yang-jo-jang
business center	비즈니스 센터	bi-jeu-ni-seu sen-teo
business school	비즈니스 스쿨	bi-jeu-ni-seu seu-kul

casino	카지노	ka-ji-no
construction	건설	geon-seol
consulting	컨설팅	keon-seol-ting

dental clinic	치과 병원	chi-gwa byeong-won
design	디자인	di-ja-in
drugstore, pharmacy	약국	yak-guk
dry cleaners	드라이 클리닝	deu-ra-i keul-li-ning
employment agency	직업 소개소	ji-geop so-gae-so

financial services	재무 서비스	jae-mu seo-bi-seu
food products	식품	sik-pum
funeral home	장례식장	jang-nye-sik-jang
furniture (e.g., house ~)	가구	ga-gu
clothing, garment	옷	ot
hotel	호텔	ho-tel

ice-cream	아이스크림	a-i-seu-keu-rim
industry (manufacturing)	산업, 공업	san-eop, gong-eop
insurance	보험	bo-heom
Internet	인터넷	in-teo-net
investments (finance)	투자	tu-ja

jeweler	보석 상인	bo-seok sang-in
jewelry	보석	bo-seok
laundry (shop)	세탁소	se-tak-so
legal advisor	법률컨설팅	beom-nyul-keon-seol-ting
light industry	경공업	gyeong-gong-eop

magazine	잡지	jap-ji
medicine	의학	ui-hak
movie theater	영화관	yeong-hwa-gwan
museum	박물관	bang-mul-gwan

news agency	통신사	tong-sin-sa
newspaper	신문	sin-mun
nightclub	나이트 클럽	na-i-teu keul-leop

oil (petroleum)	석유	seo-gyu
courier services	문서 송달 회사	mun-seo song-dal hoe-sa
pharmaceutics	의약	ui-yak
printing (industry)	인쇄산업	in-swae-san-eop
publishing house	출판사	chul-pan-sa
radio (~ station)	라디오	ra-di-o
real estate	부동산	bu-dong-san

restaurant	레스토랑	re-seu-to-rang
security company	보안 회사	bo-an hoe-sa
sports	스포츠	seu-po-cheu
stock exchange	증권거래소	jeung-gwon-geo-rae-so
store	가게, 상점	ga-ge, sang-jeom
supermarket	슈퍼마켓	syu-peo-ma-ket
swimming pool (public ~)	수영장	su-yeong-jang
tailor shop	양복점	yang-bok-jeom
television	텔레비전	tel-le-bi-jeon
theater	극장	geuk-jang
trade (commerce)	거래	geo-rae
transportation	운송	un-song
travel	관광산업	gwan-gwang-sa-neop
veterinarian	수의사	su-ui-sa
warehouse	창고	chang-go
waste collection	쓰레기 수거	sseu-re-gi su-geo

Job. Business. Part 2

83. Show. Exhibition

exhibition, show	전시회	jeon-si-hoe
trade show	상품 전시회	sang-pum jeon-si-hoe
participation	참가	cham-ga
to participate (vi)	참가하다	cham-ga-ha-da
participant (exhibitor)	참가자	cham-ga-ja
director	대표이사	dae-pyo-i-sa
organizers' office	조직위원회	jo-ji-gwi-won-hoe
organizer	조직위원회	jo-ji-gwi-won-hoe
to organize (vt)	조직하다	jo-jik-a-da
participation form	참가 신청서	cham-ga sin-cheong-seo
to fill out (vt)	작성하다	jak-seong-ha-da
details	상세	sang-se
information	정보	jeong-bo
price (cost, rate)	가격	ga-gyeok
including	포함하여	po-ham-ha-yeo
to include (vt)	포함하다	po-ham-ha-da
to pay (vi, vt)	지불하다	ji-bul-ha-da
registration fee	등록비	deung-nok-bi
entrance	입구	ip-gu
pavilion, hall	전시실	jeon-si-sil
to register (vt)	등록하다	deung-nok-a-da
badge (identity tag)	명찰	myeong-chal
booth, stand	부스	bu-seu
to reserve, to book	예약하다	ye-yak-a-da
display case	진열장	ji-nyeol-jang
spotlight	스포트라이트	seu-po-teu-ra-i-teu
design	디자인	di-ja-in
to place (put, set)	배치하다	bae-chi-ha-da
distributor	배급업자	bae-geu-beop-ja
supplier	공급자	gong-geup-ja
country	나라	na-ra
foreign (adj)	외국의	oe-gu-gui
product	제품	je-pum

association	협회	hyeo-poe
conference hall	회의장	hoe-ui-jang
congress	회의	hoe-ui
contest (competition)	컨테스트	keon-te-seu-teu

visitor (attendee)	방문객	bang-mun-gaek
to visit (attend)	방문하다	bang-mun-ha-da
customer	고객	go-gaek

84. Science. Research. Scientists

science	과학	gwa-hak
scientific (adj)	과학의	gwa-ha-gui
scientist	과학자	gwa-hak-ja
theory	이론	i-ron

axiom	공리	gong-ni
analysis	분석	bun-seok
to analyze (vt)	분석하다	bun-seok-a-da
argument (strong ~)	주장	ju-jang
substance (matter)	물질	mul-jil

hypothesis	가설	ga-seol
dilemma	딜레마	dil-le-ma
dissertation	학위 논문	ha-gwi non-mun
dogma	도그마	do-geu-ma

doctrine	학설	hak-seol
research	연구	yeon-gu
to research (vt)	연구하다	yeon-gu-ha-da
tests (laboratory ~)	실험	sil-heom
laboratory	연구실	yeon-gu-sil

method	방법	bang-beop
molecule	분자	bun-ja
monitoring	감시	gam-si
discovery (act, event)	발견	bal-gyeon

postulate	공준	gong-jun
principle	원칙	won-chik
forecast	예상	ye-sang
to forecast (vt)	예상하다	ye-sang-ha-da

synthesis	종합	jong-hap
trend (tendency)	경향	gyeong-hyang
theorem	정리	jeong-ni

teachings	가르침	ga-reu-chim
fact	사실	sa-sil
expedition	탐험	tam-heom

experiment	실험	sil-heom
academician	아카데미 회원	a-ka-de-mi hoe-won
bachelor (e.g., ~ of Arts)	학사	hak-sa
doctor (PhD)	박사	bak-sa
Associate Professor	부교수	bu-gyo-su
Master (e.g., ~ of Arts)	석사	seok-sa
professor	교수	gyo-su

Professions and occupations

85. Job search. Dismissal

job	직업	ji-geop
personnel	직원	ji-gwon
career	경력	gyeong-nyeok
prospects (chances)	전망	jeon-mang
skills (mastery)	숙달	suk-dal
selection (screening)	선발	seon-bal
employment agency	직업 소개소	ji-geop so-gae-so
résumé	이력서	
job interview	면접	myeon-jeop
vacancy, opening	결원	gyeo-rwon
salary, pay	급여, 월급	geu-byeo, wol-geup
fixed salary	고정급	go-jeong-geup
pay, compensation	급료	geum-nyo
position (job)	직위	ji-gwi
duty (of employee)	의무	ui-mu
range of duties	업무범위	eom-mu-beom-wi
busy (I'm ~)	바쁜	ba-ppeun
to fire (dismiss)	해고하다	hae-go-ha-da
dismissal	해고	hae-go
unemployment	실업	si-reop
unemployed (n)	실업자	si-reop-ja
retirement	은퇴	eun-toe
to retire (from job)	은퇴하다	eun-toe-ha-da

86. Business people

director	사장	sa-jang
manager (director)	지배인	ji-bae-in
boss	상사	sang-sa
superior	상사	sang-sa
superiors	상사	sang-sa
president	회장	hoe-jang
chairman	의장	ui-jang

deputy (substitute)	부 …	bu …
assistant	조수	jo-su
secretary	비서	bi-seo
personal assistant	개인 비서	gae-in bi-seo
businessman	사업가	sa-eop-ga
entrepreneur	사업가	sa-eop-ga
founder	설립자	seol-lip-ja
to found (vt)	설립하다	seol-li-pa-da
incorporator	설립자	seol-lip-ja
partner	파트너	pa-teu-neo
stockholder	주주	ju-ju
millionaire	백만장자	baeng-man-jang-ja
billionaire	억만장자	eong-man-jang-ja
owner, proprietor	소유자	so-yu-ja
landowner	토지 소유자	to-ji so-yu-ja
client	고객	go-gaek
regular client	단골	dan-gol
buyer (customer)	구매자	gu-mae-ja
visitor	방문객	bang-mun-gaek
professional (n)	전문가	jeon-mun-ga
expert	전문가	jeon-mun-ga
specialist	전문가	jeon-mun-ga
banker	은행가	eun-haeng-ga
broker	브로커	beu-ro-keo
cashier, teller	계산원	gye-san-won
accountant	회계사	hoe-gye-sa
security guard	보안요원	bo-a-nyo-won
investor	투자가	tu-ja-ga
debtor	채무자	chae-mu-ja
creditor	빚쟁이	bit-jaeng-i
borrower	차용인	cha-yong-in
importer	수입업자	su-i-beop-ja
exporter	수출업자	su-chu-reop-ja
manufacturer	생산자	saeng-san-ja
distributor	배급업자	bae-geu-beop-ja
middleman	중간상인	jung-gan-sang-in
consultant	컨설턴트	keon-seol-teon-teu
sales representative	판매 대리인	pan-mae dae-ri-in
agent	중개인	jung-gae-in
insurance agent	보험설계사	bo-heom-seol-gye-sa

87. Service professions

cook	요리사	yo-ri-sa
chef (kitchen chef)	주방장	ju-bang-jang
baker	제빵사	je-ppang-sa
bartender	바텐더	ba-ten-deo
waiter	웨이터	we-i-teo
waitress	웨이트리스	we-i-teu-ri-seu
lawyer, attorney	변호사	byeon-ho-sa
lawyer (legal expert)	법률고문	beom-nyul-go-mun
notary	공증인	gong-jeung-in
electrician	전기 기사	jeon-gi gi-sa
plumber	배관공	bae-gwan-gong
carpenter	목수	mok-su
masseur	안마사	an-ma-sa
masseuse	안마사	an-ma-sa
doctor	의사	ui-sa
taxi driver	택시 운전 기사	taek-si un-jeon gi-sa
driver	운전 기사	un-jeon gi-sa
delivery man	배달원	bae-da-rwon
chambermaid	객실 청소부	gaek-sil cheong-so-bu
security guard	보안요원	bo-a-nyo-won
flight attendant (fem.)	승무원	seung-mu-won
schoolteacher	선생님	seon-saeng-nim
librarian	사서	sa-seo
translator	번역가	beo-nyeok-ga
interpreter	통역가	tong-yeok-ga
guide	가이드	ga-i-deu
hairdresser	미용사	mi-yong-sa
mailman	우체부	u-che-bu
salesman (store staff)	점원	jeom-won
gardener	정원사	jeong-won-sa
domestic servant	하인	ha-in
maid (female servant)	하녀	ha-nyeo
cleaner (cleaning lady)	청소부	cheong-so-bu

88. Military professions and ranks

private	일병	il-byeong
sergeant	병장	byeong-jang

lieutenant	중위	jung-wi
captain	대위	dae-wi
major	소령	so-ryeong
colonel	대령	dae-ryeong
general	장군	jang-gun
marshal	원수	won-su
admiral	제독	je-dok
military (n)	군인	gun-in
soldier	군인	gun-in
officer	장교	jang-gyo
commander	사령관	sa-ryeong-gwan
border guard	국경 수비대원	guk-gyeong su-bi-dae-won
radio operator	무선 기사	mu-seon gi-sa
scout (searcher)	정찰병	jeong-chal-byeong
pioneer (sapper)	공병대원	gong-byeong-dae-won
marksman	사수	sa-su
navigator	항법사	hang-beop-sa

89. Officials. Priests

king	왕	wang
queen	여왕	yeo-wang
prince	왕자	wang-ja
princess	공주	gong-ju
czar	차르	cha-reu
czarina	여황제	yeo-hwang-je
president	대통령	dae-tong-nyeong
Secretary (minister)	장관	jang-gwan
prime minister	총리	chong-ni
senator	상원의원	sang-won-ui-won
diplomat	외교관	oe-gyo-gwan
consul	영사	yeong-sa
ambassador	대사	dae-sa
counsilor (diplomatic officer)	고문관	go-mun-gwan
official, functionary (civil servant)	공무원	gong-mu-won
prefect	도지사, 현감	do-ji-sa, hyeon-gam
mayor	시장	si-jang
judge	판사	pan-sa
prosecutor (e.g., district attorney)	검사	geom-sa

missionary	선교사	seon-gyo-sa
monk	수도사	su-do-sa
abbot	수도원장	su-do-won-jang
rabbi	랍비	rap-bi
vizier	고관	go-gwan
shah	샤	sya
sheikh	셰이크	sye-i-keu

90. Agricultural professions

beekeeper	양봉가	yang-bong-ga
herder, shepherd	목동	mok-dong
agronomist	농학자	nong-hak-ja
cattle breeder	목축업자	mok-chu-geop-ja
veterinarian	수의사	su-ui-sa
farmer	농부	nong-bu
winemaker	포도주 제조자	po-do-ju je-jo-ja
zoologist	동물학자	dong-mul-hak-ja
cowboy	카우보이	ka-u-bo-i

91. Art professions

actor	배우	bae-u
actress	여배우	yeo-bae-u
singer (masc.)	가수	ga-su
singer (fem.)	여가수	yeo-ga-su
dancer (masc.)	무용가	mu-yong-ga
dancer (fem.)	여성 무용가	yeo-seong mu-yong-ga
performer (masc.)	공연자	gong-yeon-ja
performer (fem.)	여성 공연자	yeo-seong gong-yeon-ja
musician	음악가	eum-ak-ga
pianist	피아니스트	pi-a-ni-seu-teu
guitar player	기타 연주자	gi-ta yeon-ju-ja
conductor (orchestra ~)	지휘자	ji-hwi-ja
composer	작곡가	jak-gok-ga
impresario	기획자	gi-hoek-ja
film director	영화감독	yeong-hwa-gam-dok
producer	제작자	je-jak-ja
scriptwriter	시나리오 작가	si-na-ri-o jak-ga
critic	미술 비평가	mi-sul bi-pyeong-ga

writer	작가	jak-ga
poet	시인	si-in
sculptor	조각가	jo-gak-ga
artist (painter)	화가	hwa-ga

juggler	저글러	jeo-geul-leo
clown	어릿광대	eo-rit-gwang-dae
acrobat	곡예사	go-gye-sa
magician	마술사	ma-sul-sa

92. Various professions

doctor	의사	ui-sa
nurse	간호사	gan-ho-sa
psychiatrist	정신과 의사	jeong-sin-gwa ui-sa
dentist	치과 의사	chi-gwa ui-sa
surgeon	외과 의사	oe-gwa ui-sa

| astronaut | 우주비행사 | u-ju-bi-haeng-sa |
| astronomer | 천문학자 | cheon-mun-hak-ja |

driver (of taxi, etc.)	운전 기사	un-jeon gi-sa
engineer (train driver)	기관사	gi-gwan-sa
mechanic	정비공	jeong-bi-gong

miner	광부	gwang-bu
worker	노동자	no-dong-ja
locksmith	자물쇠공	ja-mul-soe-gong
joiner (carpenter)	목수	mok-su
turner (lathe machine operator)	선반공	seon-ban-gong
construction worker	공사장 인부	gong-sa-jang in-bu
welder	용접공	yong-jeop-gong

professor (title)	교수	gyo-su
architect	건축가	geon-chuk-ga
historian	역사학자	yeok-sa-hak-ja
scientist	과학자	gwa-hak-ja
physicist	물리학자	mul-li-hak-ja
chemist (scientist)	화학자	hwa-hak-ja

archeologist	고고학자	go-go-hak-ja
geologist	지질학자	ji-jil-hak-ja
researcher (scientist)	연구원	yeon-gu-won

| babysitter | 애기보는 사람 | ae-gi-bo-neun sa-ram |
| teacher, educator | 교사 | gyo-sa |

| editor | 편집자 | pyeon-jip-ja |
| editor-in-chief | 편집장 | pyeon-jip-jang |

correspondent	통신원	tong-sin-won
typist (fem.)	타이피스트	ta-i-pi-seu-teu
designer	디자이너	di-ja-i-neo
computer expert	컴퓨터 전문가	keom-pyu-teo jeon-mun-ga
programmer	프로그래머	peu-ro-geu-rae-meo
engineer (designer)	엔지니어	en-ji-ni-eo
sailor	선원	seon-won
seaman	수부	su-bu
rescuer	구조자	gu-jo-ja
fireman	소방관	so-bang-gwan
police officer	경찰관	gyeong-chal-gwan
watchman	경비원	gyeong-bi-won
detective	형사	hyeong-sa
customs officer	세관원	se-gwan-won
bodyguard	경호원	gyeong-ho-won
prison guard	간수	gan-su
inspector	감독관	gam-dok-gwan
sportsman	스포츠맨	seu-po-cheu-maen
trainer, coach	코치	ko-chi
butcher	정육점 주인	jeong-yuk-jeom ju-in
cobbler (shoe repairer)	구둣방	gu-dut-bang
merchant	상인	sang-in
loader (person)	하역부	ha-yeok-bu
fashion designer	패션 디자이너	pae-syeon di-ja-i-neo
model (fem.)	모델	mo-del

93. Occupations. Social status

schoolboy	남학생	nam-hak-saeng
student (college ~)	대학생	dae-hak-saeng
philosopher	철학자	cheol-hak-ja
economist	경제 학자	gyeong-je hak-ja
inventor	발명가	bal-myeong-ga
unemployed (n)	실업자	si-reop-ja
retiree	은퇴자	eun-toe-ja
spy, secret agent	비밀요원	bi-mi-ryo-won
prisoner	죄수	joe-su
striker	파업자	pa-eop-ja
bureaucrat	관료	gwal-lyo
traveler (globetrotter)	여행자	yeo-haeng-ja

gay, homosexual (n)	동성애자	dong-seong-ae-ja
hacker	해커	hae-keo
bandit	산적	san-jeok
hit man, killer	살인 청부업자	sa-rin cheong-bu-eop-ja
drug addict	마약 중독자	ma-yak jung-dok-ja
drug dealer	마약 밀매자	ma-yak mil-mae-ja
prostitute (fem.)	매춘부	mae-chun-bu
pimp	포주	po-ju
sorcerer	마법사	ma-beop-sa
sorceress (evil ~)	여자 마법사	yeo-ja ma-beop-sa
pirate	해적	hae-jeok
slave	노예	no-ye
samurai	사무라이	sa-mu-ra-i
savage (primitive)	야만인	ya-man-in

Education

94. School

school	학교	hak-gyo
principal (headmaster)	교장	gyo-jang
pupil (boy)	남학생	nam-hak-saeng
pupil (girl)	여학생	yeo-hak-saeng
schoolboy	남학생	nam-hak-saeng
schoolgirl	여학생	yeo-hak-saeng
to teach (sb)	가르치다	ga-reu-chi-da
to learn (language, etc.)	배우다	bae-u-da
to learn by heart	암기하다	am-gi-ha-da
to learn (~ to count, etc.)	배우다	bae-u-da
to be in school	재학 중이다	jae-hak jung-i-da
to go to school	학교에 가다	hak-gyo-e ga-da
alphabet	알파벳	al-pa-bet
subject (at school)	과목	gwa-mok
classroom	교실	gyo-sil
lesson	수업	su-eop
recess	쉬는 시간	swi-neun si-gan
school bell	수업종	su-eop-jong
school desk	학교 책상	hak-gyo chaek-sang
chalkboard	칠판	chil-pan
grade	성적	seong-jeok
good grade	좋은 성적	jo-eun seong-jeok
bad grade	나쁜 성적	na-ppeun seong-jeok
to give a grade	성적을 매기다	seong-jeo-geul mae-gi-da
mistake, error	실수	sil-su
to make mistakes	실수하다	sil-su-ha-da
to correct (an error)	고치다	go-chi-da
cheat sheet	커닝 페이퍼	keo-ning pe-i-peo
homework	숙제	suk-je
exercise (in education)	연습 문제	yeon-seup mun-je
to be present	출석하다	chul-seok-a-da
to be absent	결석하다	gyeol-seok-a-da
to punish (vt)	처벌하다	cheo-beol-ha-da

punishment	벌	beol
conduct (behavior)	처신	cheo-sin
report card	성적표	seong-jeok-pyo
pencil	연필	yeon-pil
eraser	지우개	ji-u-gae
chalk	분필	bun-pil
pencil case	필통	pil-tong
schoolbag	책가방	chaek-ga-bang
pen	펜	pen
school notebook	노트	no-teu
textbook	교과서	gyo-gwa-seo
compasses	컴퍼스	keom-peo-seu
to make technical drawings	제도하다	je-do-ha-da
technical drawing	건축 도면	geon-chuk do-myeon
poem	시	si
by heart (adv)	외워서	oe-wo-seo
to learn by heart	암기하다	am-gi-ha-da
school vacation	학교 방학	bang-hak
to be on vacation	방학 중이다	bang-hak jung-i-da
test (written math ~)	필기 시험	pil-gi si-heom
essay (composition)	논술	non-sul
dictation	받아쓰기 시험	ba-da-sseu-gi si-heom
exam (examination)	시험	si-heom
to take an exam	시험을 보다	si-heo-meul bo-da
experiment (e.g., chemistry ~)	실험	sil-heom

95. College. University

academy	아카데미	a-ka-de-mi
university	대학교	dae-hak-gyo
faculty (e.g., ~ of Medicine)	교수진	gyo-su-jin
student (masc.)	대학생	dae-hak-saeng
student (fem.)	여대생	yeo-dae-saeng
lecturer (teacher)	강사	gang-sa
lecture hall, room	교실	gyo-sil
graduate	졸업생	jo-reop-saeng
diploma	졸업증	jo-reop-jeung
dissertation	학위 논문	ha-gwi non-mun
study (report)	연구	yeon-gu

laboratory	연구실	yeon-gu-sil
lecture	강의	gang-ui
coursemate	대학 동급생	dae-hak dong-geup-saeng
scholarship	장학금	jang-hak-geum
academic degree	학위	ha-gwi

96. Sciences. Disciplines

mathematics	수학	su-hak
algebra	대수학	dae-su-hak
geometry	기하학	gi-ha-hak
astronomy	천문학	cheon-mun-hak
biology	생물학	saeng-mul-hak
geography	지리학	ji-ri-hak
geology	지질학	ji-jil-hak
history	역사학	yeok-sa-hak
medicine	의학	ui-hak
pedagogy	교육학	gyo-yuk-ak
law	법학	beo-pak
physics	물리학	mul-li-hak
chemistry	화학	hwa-hak
philosophy	철학	cheol-hak
psychology	심리학	sim-ni-hak

97. Writing system. Orthography

grammar	문법	mun-beop
vocabulary	어휘	eo-hwi
phonetics	음성학	eum-seong-hak
noun	명사	myeong-sa
adjective	형용사	hyeong-yong-sa
verb	동사	dong-sa
adverb	부사	bu-sa
pronoun	대명사	dae-myeong-sa
interjection	감탄사	gam-tan-sa
preposition	전치사	jeon-chi-sa
root	어근	eo-geun
ending	어미	eo-mi
prefix	접두사	jeop-du-sa
syllable	음절	eum-jeol
suffix	접미사	jeom-mi-sa
stress mark	강세	gang-se

apostrophe	아포스트로피	a-po-seu-teu-ro-pi
period, dot	마침표	ma-chim-pyo
comma	쉼표	swim-pyo
semicolon	세미콜론	se-mi-kol-lon
colon	콜론	kol-lon
ellipsis	말줄임표	mal-ju-rim-pyo
question mark	물음표	mu-reum-pyo
exclamation point	느낌표	neu-kkim-pyo
quotation marks	따옴표	tta-om-pyo
in quotation marks	따옴표 안에	tta-om-pyo a-ne
parenthesis	괄호	gwal-ho
in parenthesis	괄호 속에	gwal-ho so-ge
hyphen	하이픈	ha-i-peun
dash	대시	jul-pyo
space (between words)	공백 문자	gong-baek mun-ja
letter	글자	geul-ja
capital letter	대문자	dae-mun-ja
vowel (n)	모음	mo-eum
consonant (n)	자음	ja-eum
sentence	문장	mun-jang
subject	주어	ju-eo
predicate	서술어	seo-su-reo
line	줄	jul
on a new line	줄을 바꾸어	ju-reul ba-kku-eo
paragraph	단락	dal-lak
word	단어	dan-eo
group of words	문구	mun-gu
expression	표현	pyo-hyeon
synonym	동의어	dong-ui-eo
antonym	반의어	ban-ui-eo
rule	규칙	gyu-chik
exception	예외	ye-oe
correct (adj)	맞는	man-neun
conjugation	활용	hwa-ryong
declension	어형 변화	eo-hyeong byeon-hwa
nominal case	격	gyeok
question	질문	jil-mun
to underline (vt)	밑줄을 긋다	mit-ju-reul geut-da
dotted line	점선	jeom-seon

98. Foreign languages

language	언어	eon-eo
foreign language	외국어	oe-gu-geo
to study (vt)	공부하다	gong-bu-ha-da
to learn (language, etc.)	배우다	bae-u-da
to read (vi, vt)	읽다	ik-da
to speak (vi, vt)	말하다	mal-ha-da
to understand (vt)	이해하다	i-hae-ha-da
to write (vt)	쓰다	sseu-da
fast (adv)	빨리	ppal-li
slowly (adv)	천천히	cheon-cheon-hi
fluently (adv)	유창하게	yu-chang-ha-ge
rules	규칙	gyu-chik
grammar	문법	mun-beop
vocabulary	어휘	eo-hwi
phonetics	음성학	eum-seong-hak
textbook	교과서	gyo-gwa-seo
dictionary	사전	sa-jeon
teach-yourself book	자습서	ja-seup-seo
phrasebook	회화집	hoe-hwa-jip
cassette, tape	테이프	te-i-peu
videotape	비디오테이프	bi-di-o-te-i-peu
CD, compact disc	씨디	ssi-di
DVD	디비디	di-bi-di
alphabet	알파벳	al-pa-bet
to spell (vt)	… 의 철자이다	… ui cheol-ja-i-da
pronunciation	발음	ba-reum
accent	악센트	ak-sen-teu
with an accent	사투리로	sa-tu-ri-ro
without an accent	억양 없이	eo-gyang eop-si
word	단어	dan-eo
meaning	의미	ui-mi
course (e.g., a French ~)	강좌	gang-jwa
to sign up	등록하다	deung-nok-a-da
teacher	강사	gang-sa
translation (process)	번역	beo-nyeok
translation (text, etc.)	번역	beo-nyeok
translator	번역가	beo-nyeok-ga
interpreter	통역가	tong-yeok-ga
polyglot	수개 국어를 말하는 사람	su-gae gu-geo-reul mal-ha-neun sa-ram
memory	기억력	gi-eong-nyeok

Rest. Entertainment. Travel

99. Trip. Travel

tourism, travel	관광	gwan-gwang
tourist	관광객	gwan-gwang-gaek
trip, voyage	여행	yeo-haeng
adventure	모험	mo-heom
trip, journey	여행	yeo-haeng
vacation	휴가	hyu-ga
to be on vacation	휴가 중이다	hyu-ga jung-i-da
rest	휴양	hyu-yang
train	기차	gi-cha
by train	기차로	gi-cha-ro
airplane	비행기	bi-haeng-gi
by airplane	비행기로	bi-haeng-gi-ro
by car	자동차로	ja-dong-cha-ro
by ship	배로	bae-ro
luggage	짐, 수하물	jim, su-ha-mul
suitcase	여행 가방	yeo-haeng ga-bang
luggage cart	수하물 카트	su-ha-mul ka-teu
passport	여권	yeo-gwon
visa	비자	bi-ja
ticket	표	pyo
air ticket	비행기표	bi-haeng-gi-pyo
guidebook	여행 안내서	yeo-haeng an-nae-seo
map (tourist ~)	지도	ji-do
area (rural ~)	지역	ji-yeok
place, site	곳	got
exotica (n)	이국	i-guk
exotic (adj)	이국적인	i-guk-jeo-gin
amazing (adj)	놀라운	nol-la-un
group	무리	mu-ri
excursion, sightseeing tour	견학, 관광	gyeon-hak, gwan-gwang
guide (person)	가이드	ga-i-deu

100. Hotel

hotel, inn	호텔	ho-tel
motel	모텔	mo-tel
three-star (~ hotel)	3성급	sam-seong-geub
five-star	5성급	o-seong-geub
to stay (in a hotel, etc.)	머무르다	meo-mu-reu-da
room	객실	gaek-sil
single room	일인실	i-rin-sil
double room	더블룸	deo-beul-lum
to book a room	방을 예약하다	bang-eul rye-yak-a-da
half board	하숙	ha-suk
full board	식사 제공	sik-sa je-gong
with bath	욕조가 있는	yok-jo-ga in-neun
with shower	샤워가 있는	sya-wo-ga in-neun
satellite television	위성 텔레비전	wi-seong tel-le-bi-jeon
air-conditioner	에어컨	e-eo-keon
towel	수건	su-geon
key	열쇠	yeol-soe
administrator	관리자	gwal-li-ja
chambermaid	객실 청소부	gaek-sil cheong-so-bu
porter, bellboy	포터	po-teo
doorman	도어맨	do-eo-maen
restaurant	레스토랑	re-seu-to-rang
pub, bar	바	ba
breakfast	아침식사	a-chim-sik-sa
dinner	저녁식사	jeo-nyeok-sik-sa
buffet	뷔페	bwi-pe
lobby	로비	ro-bi
elevator	엘리베이터	el-li-be-i-teo
DO NOT DISTURB	방해하지 마세요	bang-hae-ha-ji ma-se-yo
NO SMOKING	금연	geu-myeon

TECHNICAL EQUIPMENT. TRANSPORTATION

Technical equipment

101. Computer

computer	컴퓨터	keom-pyu-teo
notebook, laptop	노트북	no-teu-buk
to turn on	켜다	kyeo-da
to turn off	끄다	kkeu-da
keyboard	키보드	ki-bo-deu
key	키	ki
mouse	마우스	ma-u-seu
mouse pad	마우스 패드	ma-u-seu pae-deu
button	버튼	beo-teun
cursor	커서	keo-seo
monitor	모니터	mo-ni-teo
screen	화면, 스크린	hwa-myeon
hard disk	하드 디스크	ha-deu di-seu-keu
hard disk capacity	하드 디스크 용량	ha-deu di-seu-keu yong-nyang
memory	메모리	me-mo-ri
random access memory	램	raem
file	파일	pa-il
folder	폴더	pol-deo
to open (vt)	열다	yeol-da
to close (vt)	닫다	dat-da
to save (vt)	저장하다	jeo-jang-ha-da
to delete (vt)	삭제하다	sak-je-ha-da
to copy (vt)	복사하다	bok-sa-ha-da
to sort (vt)	정렬하다	jeong-nyeol-ha-da
to transfer (copy)	전송하다	jeon-song-ha-da
program	프로그램	peu-ro-geu-raem
software	소프트웨어	so-peu-teu-we-eo
programmer	프로그래머	peu-ro-geu-rae-meo
to program (vt)	프로그램을 작성하다	peu-ro-geu-rae-meul jak-seong-ha-da

hacker	해커	hae-keo
password	비밀번호	bi-mil-beon-ho
virus	바이러스	ba-i-reo-seu
to find, to detect	발견하다	bal-gyeon-ha-da
byte	바이트	ba-i-teu
megabyte	메가바이트	me-ga-ba-i-teu
data	데이터	de-i-teo
database	데이터베이스	de-i-teo-be-i-seu
cable (USB, etc.)	케이블	ke-i-beul
to disconnect (vt)	연결해제하다	yeon-gyeol-hae-je-ha-da
to connect (sth to sth)	연결하다	yeon-gyeol-ha-da

102. Internet. E-mail

Internet	인터넷	in-teo-net
browser	브라우저	beu-ra-u-jeo
search engine	검색 엔진	geom-saek gen-jin
provider	인터넷 서비스 제공자	in-teo-net seo-bi-seu je-gong-ja
webmaster	웹마스터	wem-ma-seu-teo
website	웹사이트	wep-sa-i-teu
webpage	웹페이지	wep-pe-i-ji
address (e-mail ~)	주소	ju-so
address book	주소록	ju-so-rok
mailbox	우편함	u-pyeon-ham
mail	메일	me-il
message	메시지	me-si-ji
sender	발송인	bal-song-in
to send (vt)	보내다	bo-nae-da
sending (of mail)	발송	bal-song
receiver	수신인	su-sin-in
to receive (vt)	받다	bat-da
correspondence	서신 교환	seo-sin gyo-hwan
to correspond (vi)	편지를 주고 받다	pyeon-ji-reul ju-go bat-da
file	파일	pa-il
to download (vt)	다운받다	da-un-bat-da
to create (vt)	창조하다	chang-jo-ha-da
to delete (vt)	삭제하다	sak-je-ha-da
deleted (adj)	삭제된	sak-je-doen
connection (ADSL, etc.)	연결	yeon-gyeol

speed	속도	sok-do
access	접속	jeop-sok
port (e.g., input ~)	포트	po-teu

| connection (make a ~) | 연결 | yeon-gyeol |
| to connect to ... (vi) | ··· 에 연결하다 | ... e yeon-gyeol-ha-da |

| to select (vt) | 선택하다 | seon-taek-a-da |
| to search (for ...) | ··· 를 검색하다 | ... reul geom-saek-a-da |

103. Electricity

electricity	전기	jeon-gi
electric, electrical (adj)	전기의	jeon-gi-ui
electric power plant	발전소	bal-jeon-so
energy	에너지	e-neo-ji
electric power	전력	jeol-lyeok

light bulb	전구	jeon-gu
flashlight	손전등	son-jeon-deung
street light	가로등	ga-ro-deung

light	전깃불	jeon-git-bul
to turn on	켜다	kyeo-da
to turn off	끄다	kkeu-da
to turn off the light	불을 끄다	bu-reul kkeu-da

to burn out (vi)	끊어지다	kkeu-neo-ji-da
short circuit	쇼트	syo-teu
broken wire	절단	jeol-dan
contact (electrical ~)	접촉	jeop-chok

light switch	스위치	seu-wi-chi
wall socket	소켓	so-ket
plug	플러그	peul-leo-geu
extension cord	연장 코드	yeon-jang ko-deu

fuse	퓨즈	pyu-jeu
cable, wire	전선	jeon-seon
wiring	배선	bae-seon

ampere	암페어	am-pe-eo
amperage	암페어수	am-pe-eo-su
volt	볼트	bol-teu
voltage	전압	jeon-ap

electrical device	전기기구	jeon-gi-gi-gu
indicator	쎈서	sen-seo
electrician	전기 기사	jeon-gi gi-sa
to solder (vt)	납땜하다	nap-ttaem-ha-da

| soldering iron | 납땜인두 | nap-ttaem-in-du |
| electric current | 전류 | jeol-lyu |

104. Tools

tool, instrument	공구	gong-gu
tools	공구	gong-gu
equipment (factory ~)	장비	jang-bi

hammer	망치	mang-chi
screwdriver	나사돌리개	na-sa-dol-li-gae
ax	도끼	do-kki

saw	톱	top
to saw (vt)	톱을 켜다	to-beul kyeo-da
plane (tool)	대패	dae-pae
to plane (vt)	대패질하다	dae-pae-jil-ha-da
soldering iron	납땜인두	nap-ttaem-in-du
to solder (vt)	납땜하다	nap-ttaem-ha-da

file (tool)	줄	jul
carpenter pincers	집게	jip-ge
lineman's pliers	펜치	pen-chi
chisel	끌	kkeul

drill bit	드릴 비트	deu-ril bi-teu
electric drill	전동 드릴	jeon-dong deu-ril
to drill (vi, vt)	뚫다	ttul-ta

knife	칼, 나이프	kal, na-i-peu
pocket knife	주머니칼	ju-meo-ni-kal
folding (~ knife)	접이식의	jeo-bi-si-gui
blade	칼날	kal-lal

sharp (blade, etc.)	날카로운	nal-ka-ro-un
dull, blunt (adj)	무딘	mu-din
to get blunt (dull)	무뎌지다	mu-dyeo-ji-da
to sharpen (vt)	갈다	gal-da

bolt	볼트	bol-teu
nut	너트	neo-teu
thread (of a screw)	나사산	na-sa-san
wood screw	나사못	na-sa-mot

| nail | 못 | mot |
| nailhead | 못대가리 | mot-dae-ga-ri |

ruler (for measuring)	자	ja
tape measure	줄자	jul-ja
spirit level	수준기	su-jun-gi

magnifying glass	돋보기	dot-bo-gi
measuring instrument	계측기	gye-cheuk-gi
to measure (vt)	측정하다	cheuk-jeong-ha-da
scale (of thermometer, etc.)	눈금	nun-geum

readings	판독값	pan-dok-gap
compressor	컴프레서	keom-peu-re-seo
microscope	현미경	hyeon-mi-gyeong

pump (e.g., water ~)	펌프	peom-peu
robot	로봇	ro-bot
laser	레이저	re-i-jeo

wrench	스패너	seu-pae-neo
adhesive tape	스카치 테이프	seu-ka-chi te-i-peu
glue	접착제	jeop-chak-je

sandpaper	사포	sa-po
magnet	자석	ja-seok
gloves	장갑	jang-gap

rope	밧줄	bat-jul
cord	끈	kkeun
wire (e.g., telephone ~)	전선	jeon-seon
cable	케이블	ke-i-beul

sledgehammer	슬레지해머	seul-le-ji-hae-meo
prybar	쇠지레	soe-ji-re
ladder	사다리	sa-da-ri
stepladder	접사다리	jeop-sa-da-ri

to screw (tighten)	돌려서 조이다	dol-lyeo-seo jo-i-da
to unscrew (lid, filter, etc.)	열리다	yeol-li-da
to tighten (e.g., with a clamp)	조이다	jo-i-da
to glue, to stick	붙이다	bu-chi-da
to cut (vt)	자르다	ja-reu-da

malfunction (fault)	고장	go-jang
repair (mending)	수리	su-ri
to repair, to fix (vt)	보수하다	bo-su-ha-da
to adjust (machine, etc.)	조절하다	jo-jeol-ha-da

to check (to examine)	확인하다	hwa-gin-ha-da
checking	확인	hwa-gin
readings	판독값	pan-dok-gap

reliable, solid (machine)	믿을 만한	mi-deul man-han
complex (adj)	복잡한	bok-ja-pan
to rust (get rusted)	녹이 슬다	no-gi seul-da
rusty, rusted (adj)	녹이 슨	no-gi seun
rust	녹	nok

Transportation

105. Airplane

airplane	비행기	bi-haeng-gi
air ticket	비행기표	bi-haeng-gi-pyo
airline	항공사	hang-gong-sa
airport	공항	gong-hang
supersonic (adj)	초음속의	cho-eum-so-gui
pilot	비행사	bi-haeng-sa
flight attendant (fem.)	승무원	seung-mu-won
navigator	항법사	hang-beop-sa
wings	날개	nal-gae
tail	꼬리	kko-ri
cockpit	조종석	jo-jong-seok
engine	엔진	en-jin
undercarriage (landing gear)	착륙 장치	chang-nyuk jang-chi
turbine	터빈	teo-bin
propeller	추진기	chu-jin-gi
black box	블랙박스	beul-laek-bak-seu
yoke (control column)	조종간	jo-jong-gan
fuel	연료	yeol-lyo
safety card	안전 안내서	an-jeon an-nae-seo
oxygen mask	산소 마스크	san-so ma-seu-keu
uniform	제복	je-bok
life vest	구명조끼	gu-myeong-jo-kki
parachute	낙하산	nak-a-san
takeoff	이륙	i-ryuk
to take off (vi)	이륙하다	i-ryuk-a-da
runway	활주로	hwal-ju-ro
visibility	시계	si-gye
flight (act of flying)	비행	bi-haeng
altitude	고도	go-do
air pocket	에어 포켓	e-eo po-ket
seat	자리	ja-ri
headphones	헤드폰	he-deu-pon
folding tray (tray table)	접는 테이블	jeom-neun te-i-beul
airplane window	창문	chang-mun
aisle	통로	tong-no

106. Train

train	기차, 열차	gi-cha, nyeol-cha
commuter train	통근 열차	tong-geun nyeol-cha
express train	급행 열차	geu-paeng yeol-cha
diesel locomotive	디젤 기관차	di-jel gi-gwan-cha
steam locomotive	증기 기관차	jeung-gi gi-gwan-cha
passenger car	객차	gaek-cha
dining car	식당차	sik-dang-cha
rails	레일	re-il
railroad	철도	cheol-do
railway tie	침목	chim-mok
platform (railway ~)	플랫폼	peul-laet-pom
track (~ 1, 2, etc.)	길	gil
semaphore	신호기	sin-ho-gi
station	역	yeok
engineer (train driver)	기관사	gi-gwan-sa
porter (of luggage)	포터	po-teo
car attendant	차장	cha-jang
passenger	승객	seung-gaek
conductor (ticket inspector)	검표원	geom-pyo-won
corridor (in train)	통로	tong-no
emergency brake	비상 브레이크	bi-sang beu-re-i-keu
compartment	침대차	chim-dae-cha
berth	침대	chim-dae
upper berth	윗침대	wit-chim-dae
lower berth	아래 침대	a-rae chim-dae
bed linen, bedding	침구	chim-gu
ticket	표	pyo
schedule	시간표	si-gan-pyo
information display	안내 전광판	an-nae jeon-gwang-pan
to leave, to depart	떠난다	tteo-na-da
departure (of train)	출발	chul-bal
to arrive (ab. train)	도착하다	do-chak-a-da
arrival	도착	do-chak
to arrive by train	기차로 도착하다	gi-cha-ro do-chak-a-da
to get on the train	기차에 타다	gi-cha-e ta-da
to get off the train	기차에서 내리다	gi-cha-e-seo nae-ri-da
train wreck	기차 사고	gi-cha sa-go
steam locomotive	증기 기관차	jeung-gi gi-gwan-cha

stoker, fireman	화부	hwa-bu
firebox	화실	hwa-sil
coal	석탄	seok-tan

107. Ship

| ship | 배 | bae |
| vessel | 배 | bae |

steamship	증기선	jeung-gi-seon
riverboat	강배	gang-bae
cruise ship	크루즈선	keu-ru-jeu-seon
cruiser	순양함	su-nyang-ham

| yacht | 요트 | yo-teu |
| tugboat | 예인선 | ye-in-seon |

| sailing ship | 범선 | beom-seon |
| brigantine | 쌍돛대 범선 | ssang-dot-dae beom-seon |

| ice breaker | 쇄빙선 | swae-bing-seon |
| submarine | 잠수함 | jam-su-ham |

boat (flat-bottomed ~)	보트	bo-teu
dinghy	종선	jong-seon
lifeboat	구조선	gu-jo-seon
motorboat	모터보트	mo-teo-bo-teu

captain	선장	seon-jang
seaman	수부	su-bu
sailor	선원	seon-won
crew	승무원	seung-mu-won

boatswain	갑판장	gap-pan-jang
cook	요리사	yo-ri-sa
ship's doctor	선의	seon-ui

deck	갑판	gap-pan
mast	돛대	dot-dae
sail	돛	dot

hold	화물칸	hwa-mul-kan
bow (prow)	이물	i-mul
stern	고물	go-mul
oar	노	no
screw propeller	스크루	seu-keu-ru

cabin	선실	seon-sil
wardroom	사관실	sa-gwan-sil
engine room	엔진실	en-jin-sil

| radio room | 무전실 | mu-jeon-sil |
| wave (radio) | 전파 | jeon-pa |

spyglass	망원경	mang-won-gyeong
bell	종	jong
flag	기	gi

| hawser (mooring ~) | 밧줄 | bat-jul |
| knot (bowline, etc.) | 매듭 | mae-deup |

| deckrails | 난간 | nan-gan |
| gangway | 사다리 | sa-da-ri |

anchor	닻	dat
to weigh anchor	닻을 올리다	da-cheul rol-li-da
to drop anchor	닻을 내리다	da-cheul lae-ri-da
anchor chain	닻줄	dat-jul

port (harbor)	항구	hang-gu
quay, wharf	부두	bu-du
to berth (moor)	정박시키다	jeong-bak-si-ki-da
to cast off	출항하다	chul-hang-ha-da

trip, voyage	여행	yeo-haeng
cruise (sea trip)	크루즈	keu-ru-jeu
course (route)	항로	hang-no
route (itinerary)	노선	no-seon

fairway (safe water channel)	항로	hang-no
shallows	얕은 곳	ya-teun got
to run aground	좌초하다	jwa-cho-ha-da

storm	폭풍우	pok-pung-u
signal	신호	sin-ho
to sink (vi)	가라앉다	ga-ra-an-da
SOS (distress signal)	조난 신호	jo-nan sin-ho
ring buoy	구명부환	gu-myeong-bu-hwan

108. Airport

airport	공항	gong-hang
airplane	비행기	bi-haeng-gi
airline	항공사	hang-gong-sa
air traffic controller	관제사	gwan-je-sa

departure	출발	chul-bal
arrival	도착	do-chak
to arrive (by plane)	도착하다	do-chak-a-da
departure time	출발시간	chul-bal-si-gan

arrival time	도착시간	do-chak-si-gan
to be delayed	연기되다	yeon-gi-doe-da
flight delay	항공기 지연	hang-gong-gi ji-yeon
information board	안내 전광판	an-nae jeon-gwang-pan
information	정보	jeong-bo
to announce (vt)	알리다	al-li-da
flight (e.g., next ~)	비행편	bi-haeng-pyeon
customs	세관	se-gwan
customs officer	세관원	se-gwan-won
customs declaration	세관신고서	se-gwan-sin-go-seo
to fill out the declaration	세관 신고서를 작성하다	se-gwan sin-go-seo-reul jak-seong-ha-da
passport control	여권 검사	yeo-gwon geom-sa
luggage	짐, 수하물	jim, su-ha-mul
hand luggage	휴대 가능 수하물	hyu-dae ga-neung su-ha-mul
luggage cart	수하물 카트	su-ha-mul ka-teu
landing	착륙	chang-nyuk
landing strip	활주로	hwal-ju-ro
to land (vi)	착륙하다	chang-nyuk-a-da
airstairs	승강계단	seung-gang-gye-dan
check-in	체크인	che-keu-in
check-in counter	체크인 카운터	che-keu-in ka-un-teo
to check-in (vi)	체크인하다	che-keu-in-ha-da
boarding pass	탑승권	tap-seung-gwon
departure gate	탑승구	tap-seung-gu
transit	트랜싯, 환승	teu-raen-sit, hwan-seung
to wait (vt)	기다리다	gi-da-ri-da
departure lounge	공항 라운지	gong-hang na-un-ji
to see off	배웅하다	bae-ung-ha-da
to say goodbye	작별인사를 하다	jak-byeo-rin-sa-reul ha-da

Life events

celebration, holiday	휴일	hyu-il
national day	국경일	guk-gyeong-il
public holiday	공휴일	gong-hyu-il
to commemorate (vt)	기념하다	gi-nyeom-ha-da
event (happening)	사건	sa-geon
event (organized activity)	이벤트	i-ben-teu
banquet (party)	연회	yeon-hoe
reception (formal party)	리셉션	ri-sep-syeon
feast	연회	yeon-hoe
anniversary	기념일	gi-nyeom-il
jubilee	기념일	gi-nyeom-il
to celebrate (vt)	경축하다	gyeong-chuk-a-da
New Year	새해	sae-hae
Happy New Year!	새해 복 많이 받으세요!	sae-hae bok ma-ni ba-deu-se-yo!
Santa Claus	산타클로스	san-ta-keul-lo-seu
Christmas	크리스마스	keu-ri-seu-ma-seu
Merry Christmas!	성탄을 축하합니다!	seong-ta-neul chuk-a-ham-ni-da!
Christmas tree	크리스마스트리	keu-ri-seu-ma-seu-teu-ri
fireworks (fireworks show)	불꽃놀이	bul-kkon-no-ri
wedding	결혼식	gyeol-hon-sik
groom	신랑	sil-lang
bride	신부	sin-bu
to invite (vt)	초대하다	cho-dae-ha-da
invitation card	초대장	cho-dae-jang
guest	손님	son-nim
to visit (~ your parents, etc.)	방문하다	bang-mun-ha-da
to meet the guests	손님을 맞이하다	son-ni-meul ma-ji-ha-da
gift, present	선물	seon-mul
to give (sth as present)	선물 하다	seon-mul ha-da
to receive gifts	선물 받다	seon-mul bat-da
bouquet (of flowers)	꽃다발	kkot-da-bal

congratulations	축하를	chuk-a-reul
to congratulate (vt)	축하하다	chuk-a-ha-da
greeting card	축하 카드	chuk-a ka-deu
to send a postcard	카드를 보내다	ka-deu-reul bo-nae-da
to get a postcard	카드 받다	ka-deu bat-da
toast	축배	chuk-bae
to offer (a drink, etc.)	대접하다	dae-jeo-pa-da
champagne	샴폐인	syam-pe-in
to enjoy oneself	즐기다	jeul-gi-da
merriment (gaiety)	즐거움	jeul-geo-um
joy (emotion)	기쁜, 즐거움	gi-ppeun, jeul-geo-um
dance	춤	chum
to dance (vi, vt)	춤추다	chum-chu-da
waltz	왈츠	wal-cheu
tango	탱고	taeng-go

110. Funerals. Burial

cemetery	묘지	myo-ji
grave, tomb	무덤	mu-deom
cross	십자가	sip-ja-ga
gravestone	묘석	myo-seok
fence	울타리	ul-ta-ri
chapel	채플	chae-peul
death	죽음	ju-geum
to die (vi)	죽다	juk-da
the deceased	고인	go-in
mourning	상	sang
to bury (vt)	묻다	mut-da
funeral home	장례식장	jang-nye-sik-jang
funeral	장례식	jang-nye-sik
wreath	화환	hwa-hwan
casket, coffin	관	gwan
hearse	영구차	yeong-gu-cha
shroud	수의	su-ui
funerary urn	유골 단지	yu-gol dan-ji
crematory	화장장	hwa-jang-jang
obituary	부고	bu-go
to cry (weep)	울다	ul-da
to sob (vi)	흐느껴 울다	heu-neu-kkyeo ul-da

111. War. Soldiers

platoon	소대	so-dae
company	중대	jung-dae
regiment	연대	yeon-dae
army	군대	gun-dae
division	사단	sa-dan
section, squad	분대	bun-dae
host (army)	군대	gun-dae
soldier	군인	gun-in
officer	장교	jang-gyo
private	일병	il-byeong
sergeant	병장	byeong-jang
lieutenant	중위	jung-wi
captain	대위	dae-wi
major	소령	so-ryeong
colonel	대령	dae-ryeong
general	장군	jang-gun
sailor	선원	seon-won
captain	대위	dae-wi
boatswain	갑판장	gap-pan-jang
artilleryman	포병	po-byeong
paratrooper	낙하산 부대원	nak-a-san bu-dae-won
pilot	조종사	jo-jong-sa
navigator	항법사	hang-beop-sa
mechanic	정비공	jeong-bi-gong
pioneer (sapper)	공병대원	gong-byeong-dae-won
parachutist	낙하산병	nak-a-san-byeong
reconnaissance scout	정찰대	jeong-chal-dae
sniper	저격병	jeo-gyeok-byeong
patrol (group)	순찰	sun-chal
to patrol (vt)	순찰하다	sun-chal-ha-da
sentry, guard	경비병	gyeong-bi-byeong
warrior	전사	jeon-sa
hero	영웅	yeong-ung
heroine	여걸	yeo-geol
patriot	애국자	ae-guk-ja
traitor	매국노	mae-gung-no
deserter	탈영병	ta-ryeong-byeong
to desert (vi)	탈영하다	ta-ryeong-ha-da
mercenary	용병	yong-byeong
recruit	훈련병	hul-lyeon-byeong

volunteer	지원병	ji-won-byeong
dead (n)	사망자	sa-mang-ja
wounded (n)	부상자	bu-sang-ja
prisoner of war	포로	po-ro

112. War. Military actions. Part 1

war	전쟁	jeon-jaeng
to be at war	참전하다	cham-jeon-ha-da
civil war	내전	nae-jeon

treacherously (adv)	비겁하게	bi-geo-pa-ge
declaration of war	선전 포고	seon-jeon po-go
to declare (~ war)	선포하다	seon-po-ha-da
aggression	침략	chim-nyak
to attack (invade)	공격하다	gong-gyeo-ka-da

to invade (vt)	침략하다	chim-nyak-a-da
invader	침략자	chim-nyak-ja
conqueror	정복자	jeong-bok-ja

defense	방어	bang-eo
to defend (a country, etc.)	방어하다	bang-eo-ha-da
to defend (against ...)	··· 를 방어하다	... reul bang-eo-ha-da

enemy	적	jeok
foe, adversary	원수	won-su
enemy (as adj)	적의	jeo-gui

| strategy | 전략 | jeol-lyak |
| tactics | 전술 | jeon-sul |

order	명령	myeong-nyeong
command (order)	명령	myeong-nyeong
to order (vt)	명령하다	myeong-nyeong-ha-da
mission	임무	im-mu
secret (adj)	비밀의	bi-mi-rui

battle	전투	jeon-tu
battle	전투	jeon-tu
combat	전투	jeon-tu

attack	공격	gong-gyeok
charge (assault)	돌격	dol-gyeok
to storm (vt)	습격하다	seup-gyeok-a-da
siege (to be under ~)	포위 공격	po-wi gong-gyeok

offensive (n)	공세	gong-se
to go on the offensive	공격하다	gong-gyeo-ka-da
retreat	퇴각	toe-gak

to retreat (vi)	퇴각하다	toe-gak-a-da
encirclement	포위	po-wi
to encircle (vt)	둘러싸다	dul-leo-ssa-da
bombing (by aircraft)	폭격	pok-gyeok
to drop a bomb	폭탄을 투하하다	pok-ta-neul tu-ha-ha-da
to bomb (vt)	폭격하다	pok-gyeok-a-da
explosion	폭발	pok-bal
shot	발포	bal-po
to fire (~ a shot)	쏘다	sso-da
firing (burst of ~)	사격	sa-gyeok
to aim (to point a weapon)	겨냥대다	gyeo-nyang-dae-da
to point (a gun)	총을 겨누다	chong-eul gyeo-nu-da
to hit (the target)	맞히다	ma-chi-da
to sink (~ a ship)	가라앉히다	ga-ra-an-chi-da
hole (in a ship)	구멍	gu-meong
to founder, to sink (vi)	가라앉히다	ga-ra-an-chi-da
front (war ~)	전선	jeon-seon
evacuation	철수	cheol-su
to evacuate (vt)	대피시키다	dae-pi-si-ki-da
trench	참호	cham-ho
barbwire	가시철사	ga-si-cheol-sa
barrier (anti tank ~)	장애물	jang-ae-mul
watchtower	감시탑	gam-si-tap
military hospital	군 병원	gun byeong-won
to wound (vt)	부상을 입히다	bu-sang-eul ri-pi-da
wound	부상	bu-sang
wounded (n)	부상자	bu-sang-ja
to be wounded	부상을 입다	bu-sang-eul rip-da
serious (wound)	심각한	sim-gak-an

113. War. Military actions. Part 2

captivity	사로잡힘	sa-ro-ja-pim
to take captive	포로로 하다	po-ro-ro ha-da
to be held captive	사로잡히어	sa-ro-ja-pi-eo
to be taken captive	포로가 되다	po-ro-ga doe-da
concentration camp	강제 수용소	gang-je su-yong-so
prisoner of war	포로	po-ro
to escape (vi)	탈출하다	tal-chul-ha-da
to betray (vt)	팔아먹다	pa-ra-meok-da
betrayer	배반자	bae-ban-ja

betrayal	배반	bae-ban
to execute (by firing squad)	총살하다	chong-sal-ha-da
execution (by firing squad)	총살형	chong-sal-hyeong

equipment (military gear)	군장	gun-jang
shoulder board	계급 견장	gye-geup gyeon-jang
gas mask	가스 마스크	ga-seu ma-seu-keu

field radio	군용무전기	gu-nyong-mu-jeon-gi
cipher, code	암호	am-ho
secrecy	비밀 유지	bi-mil ryu-ji
password	비밀번호	bi-mil-beon-ho

land mine	지뢰	ji-roe
to mine (road, etc.)	지뢰를 매설하다	ji-roe-reul mae-seol-ha-da
minefield	지뢰밭	ji-roe-bat

air-raid warning	공습 경보	gong-seup gyeong-bo
alarm (alert signal)	경보	gyeong-bo
signal	신호	sin-ho
signal flare	신호탄	sin-ho-tan

headquarters	본부	bon-bu
reconnaissance	정찰	jeong-chal
situation	정세	jeong-se
report	보고	bo-go
ambush	기습	gi-seup
reinforcement (of army)	강화	gang-hwa

target	과녁	gwa-nyeok
proving ground	성능 시험장	seong-neung si-heom-jang
military exercise	군사 훈련	gun-sa hul-lyeon

panic	공황	gong-hwang
devastation	파멸	pa-myeol
destruction, ruins	파피	pa-goe
to destroy (vt)	파피하다	pa-goe-ha-da

to survive (vi, vt)	살아남다	sa-ra-nam-da
to disarm (vt)	무장해제하다	mu-jang-hae-je-ha-da
to handle (~ a gun)	다루다	da-ru-da

| Attention! | 차려! | cha-ryeo! |
| At ease! | 쉬어! | swi-eo! |

act of courage	무훈	mu-hun
oath (vow)	맹세	maeng-se
to swear (an oath)	맹세하다	maeng-se-ha-da

| decoration (medal, etc.) | 훈장 | hun-jang |
| to award (give medal to) | 훈장을 주다 | hun-jang-eul ju-da |

medal	메달	me-dal
order (e.g., ~ of Merit)	훈장	hun-jang
victory	승리	seung-ni
defeat	패배	pae-bae
armistice	휴전	hyu-jeon
standard (battle flag)	기	gi
glory (honor, fame)	영광	yeong-gwang
parade	퍼레이드	peo-re-i-deu
to march (on parade)	행진하다	haeng-jin-ha-da

114. Weapons

weapons	무기	mu-gi
firearms	화기	hwa-gi
chemical weapons	화학 병기	hwa-hak byeong-gi
nuclear (adj)	핵의	hae-gui
nuclear weapons	핵무기	haeng-mu-gi
bomb	폭탄	pok-tan
atomic bomb	원자폭탄	won-ja-pok-tan
pistol (gun)	권총	gwon-chong
rifle	장총	jang-chong
submachine gun	기관단총	gi-gwan-dan-chong
machine gun	기관총	gi-gwan-chong
muzzle	총구	chong-gu
barrel	총열	chong-yeol
caliber	구경	gu-gyeong
trigger	방아쇠	bang-a-soe
sight (aiming device)	가늠자	ga-neum-ja
butt (shoulder stock)	개머리	gae-meo-ri
hand grenade	수류탄	su-ryu-tan
explosive	폭약	po-gyak
bullet	총알	chong-al
cartridge	탄약통	ta-nyak-tong
charge	화약	hwa-yak
ammunition	탄약	ta-nyak
bomber (aircraft)	폭격기	pok-gyeok-gi
fighter	전투기	jeon-tu-gi
helicopter	헬리콥터	hel-li-kop-teo
anti-aircraft gun	대공포	dae-gong-po
tank	전차	jeon-cha

artillery	대포	dae-po
gun (cannon, howitzer)	대포	dae-po
to lay (a gun)	총을 겨누다	chong-eul gyeo-nu-da
shell (projectile)	탄피	tan-pi
mortar bomb	박격포탄	bak-gyeok-po-tan
mortar	박격포	bak-gyeok-po
splinter (shell fragment)	포탄파편	po-tan-pa-pyeon
submarine	잠수함	jam-su-ham
torpedo	어뢰	eo-roe
missile	미사일	mi-sa-il
to load (gun)	장탄하다	jang-tan-ha-da
to shoot (vi)	쏘다	sso-da
to point at (the cannon)	총을 겨누다	chong-eul gyeo-nu-da
bayonet	총검	chong-geom
rapier	레이피어	re-i-pi-eo
saber (e.g., cavalry ~)	군도	gun-do
spear (weapon)	창	chang
bow	활	hwal
arrow	화살	hwa-sal
musket	머스킷	meo-seu-kit
crossbow	석궁	seok-gung

115. Ancient people

primitive (prehistoric)	원시적인	won-si-jeo-gin
prehistoric (adj)	선사시대의	seon-sa-si-dae-ui
ancient (~ civilization)	고대의	go-dae-ui
Stone Age	석기 시대	seok-gi si-dae
Bronze Age	청동기 시대	cheong-dong-gi si-dae
Ice Age	빙하 시대	bing-ha si-dae
tribe	부족	bu-jok
cannibal	식인종	si-gin-jong
hunter	사냥꾼	sa-nyang-kkun
to hunt (vi, vt)	사냥하다	sa-nyang-ha-da
mammoth	매머드	mae-meo-deu
cave	동굴	dong-gul
fire	불	bul
campfire	모닥불	mo-dak-bul
cave painting	동굴 벽화	dong-gul byeok-wa
tool (e.g., stone ax)	도구	do-gu
spear	창	chang
stone ax	돌도끼	dol-do-kki

to be at war	참전하다	cham-jeon-ha-da
to domesticate (vt)	길들이다	gil-deu-ri-da
idol	우상	u-sang
to worship (vt)	숭배하다	sung-bae-ha-da
superstition	미신	mi-sin
evolution	진화	jin-hwa
development	개발	gae-bal
disappearance (extinction)	멸종	myeol-jong
to adapt oneself	적응하다	jeo-geung-ha-da
archeology	고고학	go-go-hak
archeologist	고고학자	go-go-hak-ja
archeological (adj)	고고학의	go-go-ha-gui
excavation site	발굴 현장	bal-gul hyeon-jang
excavations	발굴	bal-gul
find (object)	발견물	bal-gyeon-mul
fragment	파편	pa-pyeon

116. Middle Ages

people (ethnic group)	민족	min-jok
peoples	민족	min-jok
tribe	부족	bu-jok
tribes	부족들	bu-jok-deul
barbarians	오랑캐	o-rang-kae
Gauls	갈리아인	gal-li-a-in
Goths	고트족	go-teu-jok
Slavs	슬라브족	seul-la-beu-jok
Vikings	바이킹	ba-i-king
Romans	로마 사람	ro-ma sa-ram
Roman (adj)	로마의	ro-ma-ui
Byzantines	비잔티움 사람들	bi-jan-ti-um sa-ram-deul
Byzantium	비잔티움	bi-jan-ti-um
Byzantine (adj)	비잔틴의	bi-jan-tin-ui
emperor	황제	hwang-je
leader, chief (tribal ~)	추장	chu-jang
powerful (~ king)	강력한	gang-nyeo-kan
king	왕	wang
ruler (sovereign)	통치자	tong-chi-ja
knight	기사	gi-sa
feudal lord	봉건 영주	bong-geon nyeong-ju
feudal (adj)	봉건적인	bong-geon-jeo-gin

vassal	봉신	bong-sin
duke	공작	gong-jak
earl	백작	baek-jak
baron	남작	nam-jak
bishop	주교	ju-gyo

armor	갑옷	ga-bot
shield	방패	bang-pae
sword	검	geom
visor	얼굴 가리개	eol-gul ga-ri-gae
chainmail	미늘 갑옷	mi-neul ga-bot
Crusade	십자군	sip-ja-gun
crusader	십자군 전사	sip-ja-gun jeon-sa

territory	영토	yeong-to
to attack (invade)	공격하다	gong-gyeo-ka-da
to conquer (vt)	정복하다	jeong-bok-a-da
to occupy (invade)	점령하다	jeom-nyeong-ha-da

siege (to be under ~)	포위 공격	po-wi gong-gyeok
besieged (adj)	포위당한	po-wi-dang-han
to besiege (vt)	포위하다	po-wi-ha-da

inquisition	이단심문	i-dan-sim-mun
inquisitor	종교 재판관	jong-gyo jae-pan-gwan
torture	고문	go-mun
cruel (adj)	잔혹한	jan-hok-an
heretic	이단자	i-dan-ja
heresy	이단으로	i-da-neu-ro

seafaring	항해	hang-hae
pirate	해적	hae-jeok
piracy	해적 행위	hae-jeok aeng-wi
boarding (attack)	널판장	neol-pan-jang
loot, booty	노획물	no-hoeng-mul
treasures	보물	bo-mul

discovery	발견	bal-gyeon
to discover (new land, etc.)	발견하다	bal-gyeon-ha-da
expedition	탐험	tam-heom

musketeer	총병	chong-byeong
cardinal	추기경	chu-gi-gyeong
heraldry	문장학	mun-jang-hak
heraldic (adj)	문장학의	mun-jang-ha-gui

117. Leader. Chief. Authorities

king	왕	wang
queen	여왕	yeo-wang

| royal (adj) | 왕족의 | wang-jo-gui |
| kingdom | 왕국 | wang-guk |

| prince | 왕자 | wang-ja |
| princess | 공주 | gong-ju |

president	대통령	dae-tong-nyeong
vice-president	부통령	bu-tong-nyeong
senator	상원의원	sang-won-ui-won

monarch	군주	gun-ju
ruler (sovereign)	통치자	tong-chi-ja
dictator	독재자	dok-jae-ja
tyrant	폭군	pok-gun
magnate	거물	geo-mul

director	사장	sa-jang
chief	추장	chu-jang
manager (director)	지배인	ji-bae-in
boss	상사	sang-sa
owner	소유자	so-yu-ja

head (~ of delegation)	책임자	chae-gim-ja
authorities	당국	dang-guk
superiors	상사	sang-sa

governor	주지사	ju-ji-sa
consul	영사	yeong-sa
diplomat	외교관	oe-gyo-gwan
mayor	시장	si-jang
sheriff	보안관	bo-an-gwan

emperor	황제	hwang-je
tsar, czar	황제	hwang-je
pharaoh	파라오	pa-ra-o
khan	칸	kan

118. Breaking the law. Criminals. Part 1

bandit	산적	san-jeok
crime	범죄	beom-joe
criminal (person)	범죄자	beom-joe-ja

thief	도둑	do-duk
to steal (vi, vt)	훔치다	hum-chi-da
stealing (larceny)	절도	jeol-do
theft	도둑질	do-duk-jil

| to kidnap (vt) | 납치하다 | nap-chi-ha-da |
| kidnapping | 유괴 | yu-goe |

kidnapper	유괴범	yu-goe-beom
ransom	몸값	mom-gap
to demand ransom	몸값을 요구하다	mom-gap-seul ryo-gu-ha-da
to rob (vt)	뺏다	ppaet-da
robber	강도	gang-do
to extort (vt)	갈취하다	gal-chwi-ha-da
extortionist	갈취자	gal-chwi-ja
extortion	갈취	gal-chwi
to murder, to kill	죽이다	ju-gi-da
murder	살인	sa-rin
murderer	살인자	sa-rin-ja
gunshot	발포	bal-po
to fire (~ a shot)	쏘다	sso-da
to shoot to death	쏘아 죽이다	sso-a ju-gi-da
to shoot (vi)	쏘다	sso-da
shooting	발사	bal-sa
incident (fight, etc.)	사건	sa-geon
fight, brawl	몸싸움	mom-ssa-um
victim	희생자	hui-saeng-ja
to damage (vt)	해치다	hae-chi-da
damage	피해	pi-hae
dead body, corpse	시신	si-sin
grave (~ crime)	중대한	jung-dae-han
to attack (vt)	공격하다	gong-gyeo-ka-da
to beat (to hit)	때리다	ttae-ri-da
to beat up	조지다	jo-ji-da
to take (rob of sth)	훔치다	hum-chi-da
to stab to death	찔러 죽이다	jjil-leo ju-gi-da
to maim (vt)	불구로 만들다	bul-gu-ro man-deul-da
to wound (vt)	부상을 입히다	bu-sang-eul ri-pi-da
blackmail	공갈	gong-gal
to blackmail (vt)	공갈하다	gong-gal-ha-da
blackmailer	공갈범	gong-gal-beom
protection racket	폭력단의 갈취 행위	pong-nyeok-dan-ui gal-chwi haeng-wi
racketeer	모리배	mo-ri-bae
gangster	갱	gaeng
mafia, Mob	마피아	ma-pi-a
pickpocket	소매치기	so-mae-chi-gi
burglar	빈집털이범	bin-jip-teo-ri-beom
smuggling	밀수입	mil-su-ip

smuggler	밀수입자	mil-su-ip-ja
forgery	위조	wi-jo
to forge (counterfeit)	위조하다	wi-jo-ha-da
fake (forged)	가짜의	ga-jja-ui

119. Breaking the law. Criminals. Part 2

rape	강간	gang-gan
to rape (vt)	강간하다	gang-gan-ha-da
rapist	강간범	gang-gan-beom
maniac	미치광이	mi-chi-gwang-i

prostitute (fem.)	매춘부	mae-chun-bu
prostitution	매춘	mae-chun
pimp	포주	po-ju

| drug addict | 마약 중독자 | ma-yak jung-dok-ja |
| drug dealer | 마약 밀매자 | ma-yak mil-mae-ja |

to blow up (bomb)	폭발하다	pok-bal-ha-da
explosion	폭발	pok-bal
to set fire	방화하다	bang-hwa-ha-da
arsonist	방화범	bang-hwa-beom

terrorism	테러리즘	te-reo-ri-jeum
terrorist	테러리스트	te-reo-ri-seu-teu
hostage	볼모	bol-mo

to swindle (deceive)	속이다	so-gi-da
swindle, deception	사기	sa-gi
swindler	사기꾼	sa-gi-kkun

to bribe (vt)	뇌물을 주다	noe-mu-reul ju-da
bribery	뇌물 수수	noe-mul su-su
bribe	뇌물	noe-mul

poison	독	dok
to poison (vt)	독살하다	dok-sal-ha-da
to poison oneself	음독하다	eum-dok-a-da

| suicide (act) | 자살 | ja-sal |
| suicide (person) | 자살자 | ja-sal-ja |

to threaten (vt)	협박하다	hyeop-bak-a-da
threat	협박	hyeop-bak
to make an attempt	살해를 꾀하다	sal-hae-reul kkoe-ha-da
attempt (attack)	미수	mi-su

| to steal (a car) | 훔치는 | hum-chi-da |
| to hijack (a plane) | 납치하다 | nap-chi-ha-da |

revenge	복수	bok-su
to avenge (get revenge)	복수하다	bok-su-ha-da

to torture (vt)	고문하다	go-mun-ha-da
torture	고문	go-mun
to torment (vt)	괴롭히다	goe-ro-pi-da

pirate	해적	hae-jeok
hooligan	난동꾼	nan-dong-kkun
armed (adj)	무장한	mu-jang-han
violence	폭력	pong-nyeok

spying (espionage)	간첩행위	gan-cheo-paeng-wi
to spy (vi)	간첩 행위를 하다	gan-cheop paeng-wi-reul ha-da

120. Police. Law. Part 1

justice	정의	jeong-ui
court (see you in ~)	법정	beop-jeong

judge	판사	pan-sa
jurors	배심원	bae-sim-won
jury trial	배심 재판	bae-sim jae-pan
to judge (vt)	재판에 부치다	jae-pan-e bu-chi-da

lawyer, attorney	변호사	byeon-ho-sa
defendant	피고	pi-go
dock	피고인석	pi-go-in-seok

charge	혐의	hyeom-ui
accused	형사 피고인	pi-go-in

sentence	형량	hyeong-nyang
to sentence (vt)	선고하다	seon-go-ha-da

guilty (culprit)	유죄	yu-joe
to punish (vt)	처벌하다	cheo-beol-ha-da
punishment	벌	beol

fine (penalty)	벌금	beol-geum
life imprisonment	종신형	jong-sin-hyeong
death penalty	사형	sa-hyeong
electric chair	전기 의자	jeon-gi ui-ja
gallows	교수대	gyo-su-dae

to execute (vt)	집행하다	ji-paeng-ha-da
execution	처형	cheo-hyeong
prison, jail	교도소	gyo-do-so
cell	감방	gam-bang

escort	호송	ho-song
prison guard	간수	gan-su
prisoner	죄수	joe-su
handcuffs	수갑	su-gap
to handcuff (vt)	수갑을 채우다	su-ga-beul chae-u-da
prison break	탈옥	ta-rok
to break out (vi)	탈옥하다	ta-rok-a-da
to disappear (vi)	사라지다	sa-ra-ji-da
to release (from prison)	출옥하다	chu-rok-a-da
amnesty	사면	sa-myeon
police	경찰	gyeong-chal
police officer	경찰관	gyeong-chal-gwan
police station	경찰서	gyeong-chal-seo
billy club	경찰봉	gyeong-chal-bong
bullhorn	메가폰	me-ga-pon
patrol car	순찰차	sun-chal-cha
siren	사이렌	sa-i-ren
to turn on the siren	사이렌을 켜다	sa-i-re-neul kyeo-da
siren call	사이렌 소리	sa-i-ren so-ri
crime scene	범죄현장	beom-joe-hyeon-jang
witness	목격자	mok-gyeok-ja
freedom	자유	ja-yu
accomplice	공범자	gong-beom-ja
to flee (vi)	달아나다	da-ra-na-da
trace (to leave a ~)	흔적	heun-jeok

121. Police. Law. Part 2

search (investigation)	조사	jo-sa
to look for ...	… 를 찾다	... reul chat-da
suspicion	혐의	hyeom-ui
suspicious (e.g., ~ vehicle)	의심스러운	ui-sim-seu-reo-un
to stop (cause to halt)	멈추다	meom-chu-da
to detain (keep in custody)	구류하다	gu-ryu-ha-da
case (lawsuit)	판례	pal-lye
investigation	조사	jo-sa
detective	형사	hyeong-sa
investigator	조사관	jo-sa-gwan
hypothesis	가설	ga-seol
motive	동기	dong-gi
interrogation	심문	sim-mun
to interrogate (vt)	신문하다	sin-mun-ha-da
to question (~ neighbors, etc.)	심문하다	sim-mun-ha-da

check (identity ~)	확인	hwa-gin
round-up	일제 검거	il-je geom-geo
search (~ warrant)	수색	su-saek
chase (pursuit)	추적	chu-jeok
to pursue, to chase	추적하다	chu-jeok-a-da
to track (a criminal)	추적하다	chu-jeok-a-da
arrest	체포	che-po
to arrest (sb)	체포하다	che-po-ha-da
to catch (thief, etc.)	붙잡다	but-jap-da
capture	체포	che-po
document	서류	seo-ryu
proof (evidence)	증거	jeung-geo
to prove (vt)	증명하다	jeung-myeong-ha-da
footprint	발자국	bal-ja-guk
fingerprints	지문	ji-mun
piece of evidence	증거물	jeung-geo-mul
alibi	알리바이	al-li-ba-i
innocent (not guilty)	무죄인	mu-joe-in
injustice	부정	bu-jeong
unjust, unfair (adj)	부당한	bu-dang-han
criminal (adj)	범죄의	beom-joe-ui
to confiscate (vt)	몰수하다	mol-su-ha-da
drug (illegal substance)	마약	ma-yak
weapon, gun	무기	mu-gi
to disarm (vt)	무장해제하다	mu-jang-hae-je-ha-da
to order (command)	명령하다	myeong-nyeong-ha-da
to disappear (vi)	사라지다	sa-ra-ji-da
law	법률	beom-nyul
legal, lawful (adj)	합법적인	hap-beop-jeo-gin
illegal, illicit (adj)	불법적인	bul-beop-jeo-gin
responsibility (blame)	책임	chae-gim
responsible (adj)	책임 있는	chae-gim in-neun

NATURE

The Earth. Part 1

122. Outer space

space	우주	u-ju
space (as adj)	우주의	u-ju-ui
outer space	우주 공간	u-ju gong-gan
world	세계	se-gye
universe	우주	u-ju
galaxy	은하	eun-ha
star	별, 항성	byeol, hang-seong
constellation	별자리	byeol-ja-ri
planet	행성	haeng-seong
satellite	인공위성	in-gong-wi-seong
meteorite	운석	un-seok
comet	혜성	hye-seong
asteroid	소행성	so-haeng-seong
orbit	궤도	gwe-do
to revolve	회전한다	hoe-jeon-han-da
(~ around the Earth)		
atmosphere	대기	dae-gi
the Sun	태양	tae-yang
solar system	태양계	tae-yang-gye
solar eclipse	일식	il-sik
the Earth	지구	ji-gu
the Moon	달	dal
Mars	화성	hwa-seong
Venus	금성	geum-seong
Jupiter	목성	mok-seong
Saturn	토성	to-seong
Mercury	수성	su-seong
Uranus	천왕성	cheon-wang-seong
Neptune	해왕성	hae-wang-seong
Pluto	명왕성	myeong-wang-seong
Milky Way	은하수	eun-ha-su
Great Bear (Ursa Major)	큰곰자리	keun-gom-ja-ri

North Star	북극성	buk-geuk-seong
Martian	화성인	hwa-seong-in
extraterrestrial (n)	외계인	oe-gye-in
alien	외계인	oe-gye-in
flying saucer	비행 접시	bi-haeng jeop-si

| spaceship | 우주선 | u-ju-seon |
| space station | 우주 정거장 | u-ju jeong-nyu-jang |

engine	엔진	en-jin
nozzle	노즐	no-jeul
fuel	연료	yeol-lyo

cockpit, flight deck	조종석	jo-jong-seok
antenna	안테나	an-te-na
porthole	현창	hyeon-chang
solar panel	태양 전지	tae-yang jeon-ji
spacesuit	우주복	u-ju-bok

| weightlessness | 무중력 | mu-jung-nyeok |
| oxygen | 산소 | san-so |

| docking (in space) | 도킹 | do-king |
| to dock (vi, vt) | 도킹하다 | do-king-ha-da |

observatory	천문대	cheon-mun-dae
telescope	망원경	mang-won-gyeong
to observe (vt)	관찰하다	gwan-chal-ha-da
to explore (vt)	탐험하다	tam-heom-ha-da

123. The Earth

the Earth	지구	ji-gu
the globe (the Earth)	지구	ji-gu
planet	행성	haeng-seong

atmosphere	대기	dae-gi
geography	지리학	ji-ri-hak
nature	자연	ja-yeon

globe (table ~)	지구의	ji-gu-ui
map	지도	ji-do
atlas	지도첩	ji-do-cheop

Europe	유럽	yu-reop
Asia	아시아	a-si-a
Africa	아프리카	a-peu-ri-ka
Australia	호주	ho-ju
America	아메리카 대륙	a-me-ri-ka dae-ryuk
North America	북아메리카	bu-ga-me-ri-ka

South America	남아메리카	nam-a-me-ri-ka
Antarctica	남극 대륙	nam-geuk dae-ryuk
the Arctic	극지방	geuk-ji-bang

124. Cardinal directions

north	북쪽	buk-jjok
to the north	북쪽으로	buk-jjo-geu-ro
in the north	북쪽에	buk-jjo-ge
northern (adj)	북쪽의	buk-jjo-gui

south	남쪽	nam-jjok
to the south	남쪽으로	nam-jjo-geu-ro
in the south	남쪽에	nam-jjo-ge
southern (adj)	남쪽의	nam-jjo-gui

west	서쪽	seo-jjok
to the west	서쪽으로	seo-jjo-geu-ro
in the west	서쪽에	seo-jjo-ge
western (adj)	서쪽의	seo-jjo-gui

east	동쪽	dong-jjok
to the east	동쪽으로	dong-jjo-geu-ro
in the east	동쪽에	dong-jjo-ge
eastern (adj)	동쪽의	dong-jjo-gui

125. Sea. Ocean

sea	바다	ba-da
ocean	대양	dae-yang
gulf (bay)	만	man
straits	해협	hae-hyeop

continent (mainland)	대륙	dae-ryuk
island	섬	seom
peninsula	반도	ban-do
archipelago	군도	gun-do

bay, cove	만	man
harbor	항구	hang-gu
lagoon	석호	seok-o
cape	곶	got

atoll	환초	hwan-cho
reef	암초	am-cho
coral	산호	san-ho
coral reef	산호초	san-ho-cho
deep (adj)	깊은	gi-peun

depth (deep water)	깊이	gi-pi
trench (e.g., Mariana ~)	해구	hae-gu
current (Ocean ~)	해류	hae-ryu
to surround (bathe)	둘러싸다	dul-leo-ssa-da
shore	해변	hae-byeon
coast	바닷가	ba-dat-ga
flow (flood tide)	밀물	mil-mul
ebb (ebb tide)	썰물	sseol-mul
shoal	모래톱	mo-rae-top
bottom (~ of the sea)	해저	hae-jeo
wave	파도	pa-do
crest (~ of a wave)	물마루	mul-ma-ru
spume (sea foam)	거품	geo-pum
hurricane	허리케인	heo-ri-ke-in
tsunami	해일	hae-il
calm (dead ~)	고요함	go-yo-ham
quiet, calm (adj)	고요한	go-yo-han
pole	극	geuk
polar (adj)	극지의	geuk-ji-ui
latitude	위도	wi-do
longitude	경도	gyeong-do
parallel	위도선	wi-do-seon
equator	적도	jeok-do
sky	하늘	ha-neul
horizon	수평선	su-pyeong-seon
air	공기	gong-gi
lighthouse	등대	deung-dae
to dive (vi)	뛰어들다	ttwi-eo-deul-da
to sink (ab. boat)	가라앉다	ga-ra-an-da
treasures	보물	bo-mul

126. Seas' and Oceans' names

Atlantic Ocean	대서양	dae-seo-yang
Indian Ocean	인도양	in-do-yang
Pacific Ocean	태평양	tae-pyeong-yang
Arctic Ocean	북극해	buk-geuk-ae
Black Sea	흑해	heuk-ae
Red Sea	홍해	hong-hae
Yellow Sea	황해	hwang-hae

White Sea	백해	baek-ae
Caspian Sea	카스피 해	ka-seu-pi hae
Dead Sea	사해	sa-hae
Mediterranean Sea	지중해	ji-jung-hae

Aegean Sea	에게 해	e-ge hae
Adriatic Sea	아드리아 해	a-deu-ri-a hae

Arabian Sea	아라비아 해	a-ra-bi-a hae
Sea of Japan	동해	dong-hae
Bering Sea	베링 해	be-ring hae
South China Sea	남중국해	nam-jung-guk-ae

Coral Sea	산호해	san-ho-hae
Tasman Sea	태즈먼 해	tae-jeu-meon hae
Caribbean Sea	카리브 해	ka-ri-beu hae

Barents Sea	바렌츠 해	ba-ren-cheu hae
Kara Sea	카라 해	ka-ra hae

North Sea	북해	buk-ae
Baltic Sea	발트 해	bal-teu hae
Norwegian Sea	노르웨이 해	no-reu-we-i hae

127. Mountains

mountain	산	san
mountain range	산맥	san-maek
mountain ridge	능선	neung-seon

summit, top	정상	jeong-sang
peak	봉우리	bong-u-ri
foot (~ of the mountain)	기슭	gi-seuk
slope (mountainside)	경사면	gyeong-sa-myeon

volcano	화산	hwa-san
active volcano	활화산	hwal-hwa-san
dormant volcano	사화산	sa-hwa-san

eruption	폭발	pok-bal
crater	분화구	bun-hwa-gu
magma	마그마	ma-geu-ma
lava	용암	yong-am
molten (~ lava)	녹은	no-geun

canyon	협곡	hyeop-gok
gorge	협곡	hyeop-gok
crevice	갈라진	gal-la-jin
pass, col	산길	san-gil
plateau	고원	go-won

cliff	절벽	jeol-byeok
hill	언덕, 작은 산	eon-deok, ja-geun san
glacier	빙하	bing-ha
waterfall	폭포	pok-po
geyser	간헐천	gan-heol-cheon
lake	호수	ho-su
plain	평원	pyeong-won
landscape	경관	gyeong-gwan
echo	메아리	me-a-ri
alpinist	등산가	deung-san-ga
rock climber	암벽 등반가	am-byeok deung-ban-ga
to conquer (in climbing)	정복하다	jeong-bok-a-da
climb (an easy ~)	등반	deung-ban

128. Mountains names

The Alps	알프스 산맥	al-peu-seu san-maek
Mont Blanc	몽블랑 산	mong-beul-lang san
The Pyrenees	피레네 산맥	pi-re-ne san-maek
The Carpathians	카르파티아 산맥	ka-reu-pa-ti-a san-maek
The Ural Mountains	우랄 산맥	u-ral san-maek
The Caucasus Mountains	코카서스 산맥	ko-ka-seo-seu san-maek
Mount Elbrus	엘브루스 산	el-beu-ru-seu san
The Altai Mountains	알타이 산맥	al-ta-i san-maek
The Tian Shan	톈샨 산맥	ten-syan san-maek
The Pamir Mountains	파미르 고원	pa-mi-reu go-won
The Himalayas	히말라야 산맥	hi-mal-la-ya san-maek
Mount Everest	에베레스트 산	e-be-re-seu-teu san
The Andes	안데스 산맥	an-de-seu san-maek
Mount Kilimanjaro	킬리만자로 산	kil-li-man-ja-ro san

129. Rivers

river	강	gang
spring (natural source)	샘	saem
riverbed (river channel)	강바닥	gang-ba-dak
basin (river valley)	유역	yu-yeok
to flow into ...	… 로 흘러가다	... ro heul-leo-ga-da
tributary	지류	ji-ryu
bank (of river)	둑	duk
current (stream)	흐름	heu-reum

| downstream (adv) | 하류로 | gang ha-ryu-ro |
| upstream (adv) | 상류로 | sang-nyu-ro |

inundation	홍수	hong-su
flooding	홍수	hong-su
to overflow (vi)	범람하다	beom-nam-ha-da
to flood (vt)	범람하다	beom-nam-ha-da

| shallow (shoal) | 얕은 곳 | ya-teun got |
| rapids | 여울 | yeo-ul |

dam	댐	daem
canal	운하	un-ha
reservoir (artificial lake)	저수지	jeo-su-ji
sluice, lock	수문	su-mun

water body (pond, etc.)	저장 수량	jeo-jang su-ryang
swamp (marshland)	늪, 소택지	neup, so-taek-ji
bog, marsh	수렁	su-reong
whirlpool	소용돌이	so-yong-do-ri

stream (brook)	개울, 시내	gae-ul, si-nae
drinking (ab. water)	마실 수 있는	ma-sil su in-neun
fresh (~ water)	민물의	min-mu-rui

| ice | 얼음 | eo-reum |
| to freeze over (ab. river, etc.) | 얼다 | eol-da |

130. Rivers' names

| Seine | 센 강 | sen gang |
| Loire | 루아르 강 | ru-a-reu gang |

Thames	템스 강	tem-seu gang
Rhine	라인 강	ra-in gang
Danube	도나우 강	do-na-u gang

Volga	볼가 강	bol-ga gang
Don	돈 강	don gang
Lena	레나 강	re-na gang

Yellow River	황허강	hwang-heo-gang
Yangtze	양자강	yang-ja-gang
Mekong	메콩 강	me-kong gang
Ganges	갠지스 강	gaen-ji-seu gang

Nile River	나일 강	na-il gang
Congo River	콩고 강	kong-go gang
Okavango River	오카방고 강	o-ka-bang-go gang

Zambezi River	잠베지 강	jam-be-ji gang
Limpopo River	림포포 강	rim-po-po gang

131. Forest

forest, wood	숲	sup
forest (as adj)	산림의	sal-li-mui
thick forest	밀림	mil-lim
grove	작은 숲	ja-geun sup
forest clearing	빈터	bin-teo
thicket	덤불	deom-bul
scrubland	관목지	gwan-mok-ji
footpath (troddenpath)	오솔길	o-sol-gil
gully	도랑	do-rang
tree	나무	na-mu
leaf	잎	ip
leaves (foliage)	나뭇잎	na-mun-nip
fall of leaves	낙엽	na-gyeop
to fall (ab. leaves)	떨어지다	tteo-reo-ji-da
branch	가지	ga-ji
bough	큰 가지	keun ga-ji
bud (on shrub, tree)	잎눈	im-nun
needle (of pine tree)	바늘	ba-neul
pine cone	솔방울	sol-bang-ul
hollow (in a tree)	구멍	gu-meong
nest	둥지	dung-ji
burrow (animal hole)	굴	gul
trunk	몸통	mom-tong
root	뿌리	ppu-ri
bark	껍질	kkeop-jil
moss	이끼	i-kki
to uproot (remove trees or tree stumps)	수목을 통제 뽑다	su-mo-geul tong-jjae ppop-da
to chop down	자르다	ja-reu-da
to deforest (vt)	삼림을 없애다	sam-ni-meul reop-sae-da
tree stump	그루터기	geu-ru-teo-gi
campfire	모닥불	mo-dak-bul
forest fire	산불	san-bul
to extinguish (vt)	끄다	kkeu-da
forest ranger	산림경비원	sal-lim-gyeong-bi-won

protection	보호	bo-ho
to protect (~ nature)	보호하다	bo-ho-ha-da
poacher	밀렵자	mil-lyeop-ja
steel trap	덫	deot

| to gather, to pick (vt) | 따다 | tta-da |
| to lose one's way | 길을 잃다 | gi-reul ril-ta |

132. Natural resources

natural resources	천연 자원	cheo-nyeon ja-won
deposits	매장량	mae-jang-nyang
field (e.g., oilfield)	지역	ji-yeok

to mine (extract)	채광하다	chae-gwang-ha-da
mining (extraction)	막장일	mak-jang-il
ore	광석	gwang-seok
mine (e.g., for coal)	광산	gwang-san
shaft (mine ~)	갱도	gaeng-do
miner	광부	gwang-bu

| gas (natural ~) | 가스 | ga-seu |
| gas pipeline | 가스관 | ga-seu-gwan |

oil (petroleum)	석유	seo-gyu
oil pipeline	석유 파이프라인	seo-gyu pa-i-peu-ra-in
oil well	유정	yu-jeong
derrick (tower)	유정탑	yu-jeong-tap
tanker	유조선	yu-jo-seon

sand	모래	mo-rae
limestone	석회석	seok-oe-seok
gravel	자갈	ja-gal
peat	토탄	to-tan
clay	점토	jeom-to
coal	석탄	seok-tan

iron (ore)	철	cheol
gold	금	geum
silver	은	eun
nickel	니켈	ni-kel
copper	구리	gu-ri

zinc	아연	a-yeon
manganese	망간	mang-gan
mercury	수은	su-eun
lead	납	nap

| mineral | 광물 | gwang-mul |
| crystal | 수정 | su-jeong |

| marble | 대리석 | dae-ri-seok |
| uranium | 우라늄 | u-ra-nyum |

The Earth. Part 2

133. Weather

weather	날씨	nal-ssi
weather forecast	일기 예보	il-gi ye-bo
temperature	온도	on-do
thermometer	온도계	on-do-gye
barometer	기압계	gi-ap-gye
humidity	습함, 습기	seu-pam, seup-gi
heat (extreme ~)	더위	deo-wi
hot (torrid)	더운	deo-un
it's hot	덥다	deop-da
it's warm	따뜻하다	tta-tteu-ta-da
warm (moderately hot)	따뜻한	tta-tteu-tan
it's cold	춥다	chup-da
cold (adj)	추운	chu-un
sun	해	hae
to shine (vi)	빛나다	bin-na-da
sunny (day)	화창한	hwa-chang-han
to come up (vi)	뜨다	tteu-da
to set (vi)	지다	ji-da
cloud	구름	gu-reum
cloudy (adj)	구름의	gu-reum-ui
somber (gloomy)	흐린	heu-rin
rain	비	bi
it's raining	비가 오다	bi-ga o-da
rainy (~ day, weather)	비가 오는	bi-ga o-neun
to drizzle (vi)	이슬비가 내리다	i-seul-bi-ga nae-ri-da
pouring rain	억수	eok-su
downpour	호우	ho-u
heavy (e.g., ~ rain)	심한	sim-han
puddle	웅덩이	ung-deong-i
to get wet (in rain)	젖다	jeot-da
fog (mist)	안개	an-gae
foggy	안개가 자욱한	an-gae-ga ja-uk-an
snow	눈	nun
it's snowing	눈이 오다	nun-i o-da

134. Severe weather. Natural disasters

thunderstorm	뇌우	noe-u
lightning (~ strike)	번개	beon-gae
to flash (vi)	번쩍이다	beon-jjeo-gi-da
thunder	천둥	cheon-dung
to thunder (vi)	천둥이 치다	cheon-dung-i chi-da
it's thundering	천둥이 치다	cheon-dung-i chi-da
hail	싸락눈	ssa-rang-nun
it's hailing	싸락눈이 내리다	ssa-rang-nun-i nae-ri-da
to flood (vt)	범람하다	beom-nam-ha-da
flood, inundation	홍수	hong-su
earthquake	지진	ji-jin
tremor, quake	진동	jin-dong
epicenter	진앙	jin-ang
eruption	폭발	pok-bal
lava	용암	yong-am
twister	회오리바람	hoe-o-ri-ba-ram
tornado	토네이도	to-ne-i-do
typhoon	태풍	tae-pung
hurricane	허리케인	heo-ri-ke-in
storm	폭풍우	pok-pung-u
tsunami	해일	hae-il
fire (accident)	불	bul
disaster	재해	jae-hae
meteorite	운석	un-seok
avalanche	눈사태	nun-sa-tae
snowslide	눈사태	nun-sa-tae
blizzard	눈보라	nun-bo-ra
snowstorm	눈보라	nun-bo-ra

Fauna

135. Mammals. Predators

predator	육식 동물	yuk-sik dong-mul
tiger	호랑이	ho-rang-i
lion	사자	sa-ja
wolf	이리	i-ri
fox	여우	yeo-u
jaguar	재규어	jae-gyu-eo
leopard	표범	pyo-beom
cheetah	치타	chi-ta
puma	퓨마	pyu-ma
snow leopard	눈표범	nun-pyo-beom
lynx	스라소니	seu-ra-so-ni
coyote	코요테	ko-yo-te
jackal	재칼	jae-kal
hyena	하이에나	ha-i-e-na

136. Wild animals

animal	동물	dong-mul
beast (animal)	짐승	jim-seung
squirrel	다람쥐	da-ram-jwi
hedgehog	고슴도치	go-seum-do-chi
hare	토끼	to-kki
rabbit	굴토끼	gul-to-kki
badger	오소리	o-so-ri
raccoon	너구리	neo-gu-ri
hamster	햄스터	haem-seu-teo
marmot	마멋	ma-meot
mole	두더지	du-deo-ji
mouse	생쥐	saeng-jwi
rat	시궁쥐	si-gung-jwi
bat	박쥐	bak-jwi
ermine	북방족제비	buk-bang-jok-je-bi
sable	검은담비	geo-meun-dam-bi

| marten | 담비 | dam-bi |
| mink | 밍크 | ming-keu |

| beaver | 비버 | bi-beo |
| otter | 수달 | su-dal |

horse	말	mal
moose	엘크, 무스	el-keu, mu-seu
deer	사슴	sa-seum
camel	낙타	nak-ta

bison	미국들소	mi-guk-deul-so
aurochs	유럽들소	yu-reop-deul-so
buffalo	물소	mul-so

zebra	얼룩말	eol-lung-mal
antelope	영양	yeong-yang
roe deer	노루	no-ru
fallow deer	다마사슴	da-ma-sa-seum
chamois	샤모아	sya-mo-a
wild boar	멧돼지	met-dwae-ji

whale	고래	go-rae
seal	바다표범	ba-da-pyo-beom
walrus	바다코끼리	ba-da-ko-kki-ri
fur seal	물개	mul-gae
dolphin	돌고래	dol-go-rae

bear	곰	gom
polar bear	북극곰	buk-geuk-gom
panda	판다	pan-da

monkey	원숭이	won-sung-i
chimpanzee	침팬지	chim-paen-ji
orangutan	오랑우탄	o-rang-u-tan
gorilla	고릴라	go-ril-la
macaque	마카크	ma-ka-keu
gibbon	긴팔원숭이	gin-pa-rwon-sung-i

| elephant | 코끼리 | ko-kki-ri |
| rhinoceros | 코뿔소 | ko-ppul-so |

| giraffe | 기린 | gi-rin |
| hippopotamus | 하마 | ha-ma |

| kangaroo | 캥거루 | kaeng-geo-ru |
| koala (bear) | 코알라 | ko-al-la |

mongoose	몽구스	mong-gu-seu
chinchilla	친칠라	chin-chil-la
skunk	스컹크	seu-keong-keu
porcupine	호저	ho-jeo

137. Domestic animals

cat	고양이	go-yang-i
tomcat	수고양이	su-go-yang-i
horse	말	mal
stallion (male horse)	수말, 종마	su-mal, jong-ma
mare	암말	am-mal
cow	암소	am-so
bull	황소	hwang-so
ox	수소	su-so
sheep (ewe)	양, 암양	yang, a-myang
ram	수양	su-yang
goat	염소	yeom-so
billy goat, he-goat	숫염소	sun-nyeom-so
donkey	당나귀	dang-na-gwi
mule	노새	no-sae
pig, hog	돼지	dwae-ji
piglet	돼지 새끼	dwae-ji sae-kki
rabbit	집토끼	jip-to-kki
hen (chicken)	암탉	am-tak
rooster	수탉	su-tak
duck	집오리	ji-bo-ri
drake	수오리	su-o-ri
goose	집거위	jip-geo-wi
tom turkey, gobbler	수칠면조	su-chil-myeon-jo
turkey (hen)	칠면조	chil-myeon-jo
domestic animals	가축	ga-chuk
tame (e.g., ~ hamster)	길들여진	gil-deu-ryeo-jin
to tame (vt)	길들이다	gil-deu-ri-da
to breed (vt)	사육하다, 기르다	sa-yuk-a-da, gi-reu-da
farm	농장	nong-jang
poultry	가금	ga-geum
cattle	가축	ga-chuk
herd (cattle)	떼	tte
stable	마구간	ma-gu-gan
pigpen	돼지 우리	dwae-ji u-ri
cowshed	외양간	oe-yang-gan
rabbit hutch	토끼장	to-kki-jang
hen house	닭장	dak-jang

138. Birds

bird	새	sae
pigeon	비둘기	bi-dul-gi
sparrow	참새	cham-sae
tit (great tit)	박새	bak-sae
magpie	까치	kka-chi
raven	갈가마귀	gal-ga-ma-gwi
crow	까마귀	kka-ma-gwi
jackdaw	갈가마귀	gal-ga-ma-gwi
rook	떼까마귀	ttae-kka-ma-gwi
duck	오리	o-ri
goose	거위	geo-wi
pheasant	꿩	kkwong
eagle	독수리	dok-su-ri
hawk	매	mae
falcon	매	mae
vulture	독수리, 콘도르	dok-su-ri, kon-do-reu
condor (Andean ~)	콘도르	kon-do-reu
swan	백조	baek-jo
crane	두루미	du-ru-mi
stork	황새	hwang-sae
parrot	앵무새	aeng-mu-sae
hummingbird	벌새	beol-sae
peacock	공작	gong-jak
ostrich	타조	ta-jo
heron	왜가리	wae-ga-ri
flamingo	플라밍고	peul-la-ming-go
pelican	펠리컨	pel-li-keon
nightingale	나이팅게일	na-i-ting-ge-il
swallow	제비	je-bi
thrush	지빠귀	ji-ppa-gwi
song thrush	노래지빠귀	no-rae-ji-ppa-gwi
blackbird	대륙검은지빠귀	dae-ryuk-geo-meun-ji-ppa-gwi
swift	칼새	kal-sae
lark	종다리	jong-da-ri
quail	메추라기	me-chu-ra-gi
woodpecker	딱따구리	ttak-tta-gu-ri
cuckoo	뻐꾸기	ppeo-kku-gi
owl	올빼미	ol-ppae-mi

eagle owl	수리부엉이	su-ri-bu-eong-i
wood grouse	큰뇌조	keun-noe-jo
black grouse	멧닭	met-dak
partridge	자고	ja-go
starling	찌르레기	jji-reu-re-gi
canary	카나리아	ka-na-ri-a
chaffinch	되새	doe-sae
bullfinch	피리새	pi-ri-sae
seagull	갈매기	gal-mae-gi
albatross	신천옹	sin-cheon-ong
penguin	펭귄	peng-gwin

139. Fish. Marine animals

bream	도미류	do-mi-ryu
carp	잉어	ing-eo
perch	농어의 일종	nong-eo-ui il-jong
catfish	메기	me-gi
pike	북부민물꼬치고기	buk-bu-min-mul-kko-chi-go-gi
salmon	연어	yeon-eo
sturgeon	철갑상어	cheol-gap-sang-eo
herring	청어	cheong-eo
Atlantic salmon	대서양 연어	dae-seo-yang yeon-eo
mackerel	고등어	go-deung-eo
flatfish	넙치	neop-chi
cod	대구	dae-gu
tuna	참치	cham-chi
trout	송어	song-eo
eel	뱀장어	baem-jang-eo
electric ray	시끈가오리	si-kkeun-ga-o-ri
moray eel	곰치	gom-chi
piranha	피라니아	pi-ra-ni-a
shark	상어	sang-eo
dolphin	돌고래	dol-go-rae
whale	고래	go-rae
crab	게	ge
jellyfish	해파리	hae-pa-ri
octopus	낙지	nak-ji
starfish	불가사리	bul-ga-sa-ri
sea urchin	성게	seong-ge

seahorse	해마	hae-ma
oyster	굴	gul
shrimp	새우	sae-u
lobster	바닷가재	ba-dat-ga-jae
spiny lobster	대하	dae-ha

140. Amphibians. Reptiles

snake	뱀	baem
venomous (snake)	독이 있는	do-gi in-neun
viper	살무사	sal-mu-sa
cobra	코브라	ko-beu-ra
python	비단뱀	bi-dan-baem
boa	보아	bo-a
grass snake	풀뱀	pul-baem
rattle snake	방울뱀	bang-ul-baem
anaconda	아나콘다	a-na-kon-da
lizard	도마뱀	do-ma-baem
iguana	이구아나	i-gu-a-na
salamander	도롱뇽	do-rong-nyong
chameleon	카멜레온	ka-mel-le-on
scorpion	전갈	jeon-gal
turtle	거북	geo-buk
frog	개구리	gae-gu-ri
toad	두꺼비	du-kkeo-bi
crocodile	악어	a-geo

141. Insects

insect, bug	곤충	gon-chung
butterfly	나비	na-bi
ant	개미	gae-mi
fly	파리	pa-ri
mosquito	모기	mo-gi
beetle	딱정벌레	ttak-jeong-beol-le
wasp	말벌	mal-beol
bee	꿀벌	kkul-beol
bumblebee	호박벌	ho-bak-beol
gadfly (botfly)	쇠파리	soe-pa-ri
spider	거미	geo-mi
spiderweb	거미줄	geo-mi-jul
dragonfly	잠자리	jam-ja-ri

grasshopper	메뚜기	me-ttu-gi
moth (night butterfly)	나방	na-bang
cockroach	바퀴벌레	ba-kwi-beol-le
tick	진드기	jin-deu-gi
flea	벼룩	byeo-ruk
midge	깔따구	kkal-tta-gu
locust	메뚜기	me-ttu-gi
snail	달팽이	dal-paeng-i
cricket	귀뚜라미	gwi-ttu-ra-mi
lightning bug	개똥벌레	gae-ttong-beol-le
ladybug	무당벌레	mu-dang-beol-le
cockchafer	왕풍뎅이	wang-pung-deng-i
leech	거머리	geo-meo-ri
caterpillar	애벌레	ae-beol-le
earthworm	지렁이	ji-reong-i
larva	애벌레	ae-beol-le

Flora

142. Trees

tree	나무	na-mu
deciduous (adj)	낙엽수의	na-gyeop-su-ui
coniferous (adj)	침엽수의	chi-myeop-su-ui
evergreen (adj)	상록의	sang-no-gui
apple tree	사과나무	sa-gwa-na-mu
pear tree	배나무	bae-na-mu
cherry tree	벚나무	beon-na-mu
plum tree	자두나무	ja-du-na-mu
birch	자작나무	ja-jang-na-mu
oak	오크	o-keu
linden tree	보리수	bo-ri-su
aspen	사시나무	sa-si-na-mu
maple	단풍나무	dan-pung-na-mu
spruce	가문비나무	ga-mun-bi-na-mu
pine	소나무	so-na-mu
larch	낙엽송	na-gyeop-song
fir tree	전나무	jeon-na-mu
cedar	시다	si-da
poplar	포플러	po-peul-leo
rowan	마가목	ma-ga-mok
willow	버드나무	beo-deu-na-mu
alder	오리나무	o-ri-na-mu
beech	너도밤나무	neo-do-bam-na-mu
elm	느릅나무	neu-reum-na-mu
ash (tree)	물푸레나무	mul-pu-re-na-mu
chestnut	밤나무	bam-na-mu
magnolia	목련	mong-nyeon
palm tree	야자나무	ya-ja-na-mu
cypress	사이프러스	sa-i-peu-reo-seu
mangrove	맹그로브	maeng-geu-ro-beu
baobab	바오밥나무	ba-o-bam-na-mu
eucalyptus	유칼립투스	yu-kal-lip-tu-seu
sequoia	세쿼이아	se-kwo-i-a

143. Shrubs

bush	덤불	deom-bul
shrub	관목	gwan-mok
grapevine	포도 덩굴	po-do deong-gul
vineyard	포도밭	po-do-bat
raspberry bush	라즈베리	ra-jeu-be-ri
redcurrant bush	레드커런트 나무	re-deu-keo-reon-teu na-mu
gooseberry bush	구스베리 나무	gu-seu-be-ri na-mu
acacia	아카시아	a-ka-si-a
barberry	매자나무	mae-ja-na-mu
jasmine	재스민	jae-seu-min
juniper	두송	du-song
rosebush	장미 덤불	jang-mi deom-bul
dog rose	찔레나무	jjil-le-na-mu

144. Fruits. Berries

apple	사과	sa-gwa
pear	배	bae
plum	자두	ja-du
strawberry (garden ~)	딸기	ttal-gi
sour cherry	신양	si-nyang
sweet cherry	양벚나무	yang-beon-na-mu
grape	포도	po-do
raspberry	라즈베리	ra-jeu-be-ri
blackcurrant	블랙커렌트	beul-laek-keo-ren-teu
redcurrant	레드커렌트	re-deu-keo-ren-teu
gooseberry	구스베리	gu-seu-be-ri
cranberry	크랜베리	keu-raen-be-ri
orange	오렌지	o-ren-ji
mandarin	귤	gyul
pineapple	파인애플	pa-in-ae-peul
banana	바나나	ba-na-na
date	대추야자	dae-chu-ya-ja
lemon	레몬	re-mon
apricot	살구	sal-gu
peach	복숭아	bok-sung-a
kiwi	키위	ki-wi
grapefruit	자몽	ja-mong

berry	장과	jang-gwa
berries	장과류	jang-gwa-ryu
cowberry	월귤나무	wol-gyul-la-mu
wild strawberry	야생딸기	ya-saeng-ttal-gi
bilberry	빌베리	bil-be-ri

145. Flowers. Plants

flower	꽃	kkot
bouquet (of flowers)	꽃다발	kkot-da-bal
rose (flower)	장미	jang-mi
tulip	튤립	tyul-lip
carnation	카네이션	ka-ne-i-syeon
gladiolus	글라디올러스	geul-la-di-ol-leo-seu
cornflower	수레국화	su-re-guk-wa
harebell	실잔대	sil-jan-dae
dandelion	민들레	min-deul-le
camomile	캐모마일	kae-mo-ma-il
aloe	알로에	al-lo-e
cactus	선인장	seon-in-jang
rubber plant, ficus	고무나무	go-mu-na-mu
lily	백합	baek-ap
geranium	제라늄	je-ra-nyum
hyacinth	히아신스	hi-a-sin-seu
mimosa	미모사	mi-mo-sa
narcissus	수선화	su-seon-hwa
nasturtium	한련	hal-lyeon
orchid	난초	nan-cho
peony	모란	mo-ran
violet	바이올렛	ba-i-ol-let
pansy	팬지	paen-ji
forget-me-not	물망초	mul-mang-cho
daisy	데이지	de-i-ji
poppy	양귀비	yang-gwi-bi
hemp	삼	sam
mint	박하	bak-a
lily of the valley	은방울꽃	eun-bang-ul-kkot
snowdrop	스노드롭	seu-no-deu-rop
nettle	쐐기풀	sswae-gi-pul
sorrel	수영	su-yeong

water lily	수련	su-ryeon
fern	고사리	go-sa-ri
lichen	이끼	i-kki

greenhouse (tropical ~)	온실	on-sil
lawn	잔디	jan-di
flowerbed	꽃밭	kkot-bat

plant	식물	sing-mul
grass	풀	pul
blade of grass	풀잎	pu-rip

leaf	잎	ip
petal	꽃잎	kko-chip
stem	줄기	jul-gi
tuber	구근	gu-geun

| young plant (shoot) | 새싹 | sae-ssak |
| thorn | 가시 | ga-si |

to blossom (vi)	피우다	pi-u-da
to fade, to wither	시들다	si-deul-da
smell (odor)	향기	hyang-gi
to cut (flowers)	자르다	ja-reu-da
to pick (a flower)	따다	tta-da

146. Cereals, grains

grain	곡물	gong-mul
cereal crops	곡류	gong-nyu
ear (of barley, etc.)	이삭	i-sak

wheat	밀	mil
rye	호밀	ho-mil
oats	귀리	gwi-ri
millet	수수, 기장	su-su, gi-jang
barley	보리	bo-ri

corn	옥수수	ok-su-su
rice	쌀	ssal
buckwheat	메밀	me-mil

pea plant	완두	wan-du
kidney bean	강낭콩	gang-nang-kong
soy	콩	kong
lentil	렌즈콩	ren-jeu-kong
beans (pulse crops)	콩	kong

COUNTRIES. NATIONALITIES

147. Western Europe

Europe	유럽	yu-reop
European Union	유럽 연합	yu-reop byeon-hap
Austria	오스트리아	o-seu-teu-ri-a
Great Britain	영국	yeong-guk
England	잉글랜드	ing-geul-laen-deu
Belgium	벨기에	bel-gi-e
Germany	독일	do-gil
Netherlands	네덜란드	ne-deol-lan-deu
Holland	네덜란드	ne-deol-lan-deu
Greece	그리스	geu-ri-seu
Denmark	덴마크	den-ma-keu
Ireland	아일랜드	a-il-laen-deu
Iceland	아이슬란드	a-i-seul-lan-deu
Spain	스페인	seu-pe-in
Italy	이탈리아	i-tal-li-a
Cyprus	키프로스	ki-peu-ro-seu
Malta	몰타	mol-ta
Norway	노르웨이	no-reu-we-i
Portugal	포르투갈	po-reu-tu-gal
Finland	핀란드	pil-lan-deu
France	프랑스	peu-rang-seu
Sweden	스웨덴	seu-we-den
Switzerland	스위스	seu-wi-seu
Scotland	스코틀랜드	seu-ko-teul-laen-deu
Vatican	바티칸	ba-ti-kan
Liechtenstein	리히텐슈타인	ri-hi-ten-syu-ta-in
Luxembourg	룩셈부르크	ruk-sem-bu-reu-keu
Monaco	모나코	mo-na-ko

148. Central and Eastern Europe

Albania	알바니아	al-ba-ni-a
Bulgaria	불가리아	bul-ga-ri-a
Hungary	헝가리	heong-ga-ri

Latvia	라트비아	ra-teu-bi-a
Lithuania	리투아니아	ri-tu-a-ni-a
Poland	폴란드	pol-lan-deu

Romania	루마니아	ru-ma-ni-a
Serbia	세르비아	se-reu-bi-a
Slovakia	슬로바키아	seul-lo-ba-ki-a

Croatia	크로아티아	keu-ro-a-ti-a
Czech Republic	체코	che-ko
Estonia	에스토니아	e-seu-to-ni-a

Bosnia and Herzegovina	보스니아 헤르체코비나	bo-seu-ni-a he-reu-che-ko-bi-na
Macedonia (Republic of ~)	마케도니아	ma-ke-do-ni-a
Slovenia	슬로베니아	seul-lo-be-ni-a
Montenegro	몬테네그로	mon-te-ne-geu-ro

149. Former USSR countries

| Azerbaijan | 아제르바이잔 | a-je-reu-ba-i-jan |
| Armenia | 아르메니아 | a-reu-me-ni-a |

Belarus	벨로루시	bel-lo-ru-si
Georgia	그루지야	geu-ru-ji-ya
Kazakhstan	카자흐스탄	ka-ja-heu-seu-tan
Kirghizia	키르기스스탄	ki-reu-gi-seu-seu-tan
Moldova, Moldavia	몰도바	mol-do-ba

| Russia | 러시아 | reo-si-a |
| Ukraine | 우크라이나 | u-keu-ra-i-na |

Tajikistan	타지키스탄	ta-ji-ki-seu-tan
Turkmenistan	투르크메니스탄	tu-reu-keu-me-ni-seu-tan
Uzbekistan	우즈베키스탄	u-jeu-be-ki-seu-tan

150. Asia

Asia	아시아	a-si-a
Vietnam	베트남	be-teu-nam
India	인도	in-do
Israel	이스라엘	i-seu-ra-el

China	중국	jung-guk
Lebanon	레바논	re-ba-non
Mongolia	몽골	mong-gol
Malaysia	말레이시아	mal-le-i-si-a
Pakistan	파키스탄	pa-ki-seu-tan

Saudi Arabia	사우디아라비아	sa-u-di-a-ra-bi-a
Thailand	태국	tae-guk
Taiwan	대만	dae-man
Turkey	터키	teo-ki
Japan	일본	il-bon
Afghanistan	아프가니스탄	a-peu-ga-ni-seu-tan
Bangladesh	방글라데시	bang-geul-la-de-si
Indonesia	인도네시아	in-do-ne-si-a
Jordan	요르단	yo-reu-dan
Iraq	이라크	i-ra-keu
Iran	이란	i-ran
Cambodia	캄보디아	kam-bo-di-a
Kuwait	쿠웨이트	ku-we-i-teu
Laos	라오스	ra-o-seu
Myanmar	미얀마	mi-yan-ma
Nepal	네팔	ne-pal
United Arab Emirates	아랍에미리트	a-ra-be-mi-ri-teu
Syria	시리아	si-ri-a
Palestine	팔레스타인	pal-le-seu-ta-in
South Korea	한국	han-guk
North Korea	북한	buk-an

151. North America

United States of America	미국	mi-guk
Canada	캐나다	kae-na-da
Mexico	멕시코	mek-si-ko

152. Central and South America

Argentina	아르헨티나	a-reu-hen-ti-na
Brazil	브라질	beu-ra-jil
Colombia	콜롬비아	kol-lom-bi-a
Cuba	쿠바	ku-ba
Chile	칠레	chil-le
Bolivia	볼리비아	bol-li-bi-a
Venezuela	베네수엘라	be-ne-su-el-la
Paraguay	파라과이	pa-ra-gwa-i
Peru	페루	pe-ru
Suriname	수리남	su-ri-nam
Uruguay	우루과이	u-ru-gwa-i
Ecuador	에콰도르	e-kwa-do-reu

| The Bahamas | 바하마 | ba-ha-ma |
| Haiti | 아이티 | a-i-ti |

Dominican Republic	도미니카 공화국	do-mi-ni-ka gong-hwa-guk
Panama	파나마	pa-na-ma
Jamaica	자메이카	ja-me-i-ka

153. Africa

Egypt	이집트	i-jip-teu
Morocco	모로코	mo-ro-ko
Tunisia	튀니지	twi-ni-ji

Ghana	가나	ga-na
Zanzibar	잔지바르	jan-ji-ba-reu
Kenya	케냐	ke-nya
Libya	리비아	ri-bi-a
Madagascar	마다가스카르	ma-da-ga-seu-ka-reu

Namibia	나미비아	na-mi-bi-a
Senegal	세네갈	se-ne-gal
Tanzania	탄자니아	tan-ja-ni-a
South Africa	남아프리카 공화국	nam-a-peu-ri-ka gong-hwa-guk

154. Australia. Oceania

| Australia | 호주 | ho-ju |
| New Zealand | 뉴질랜드 | nyu-jil-laen-deu |

| Tasmania | 태즈메이니아 | tae-jeu-me-i-ni-a |
| French Polynesia | 폴리네시아 | pol-li-ne-si-a |

155. Cities

Amsterdam	암스테르담	am-seu-te-reu-dam
Ankara	앙카라	ang-ka-ra
Athens	아테네	a-te-ne
Baghdad	바그다드	ba-geu-da-deu
Bangkok	방콕	bang-kok

Barcelona	바르셀로나	ba-reu-sel-lo-na
Beijing	베이징	be-i-jing
Beirut	베이루트	be-i-ru-teu
Berlin	베를린	be-reul-lin
Bonn	본	bon

Bordeaux	보르도	bo-reu-do
Bratislava	브라티슬라바	beu-ra-ti-seul-la-ba
Brussels	브뤼셀	beu-rwi-sel
Bucharest	부쿠레슈티	bu-ku-re-syu-ti
Budapest	부다페스트	bu-da-pe-seu-teu
Cairo	카이로	ka-i-ro

Chicago	시카고	si-ka-go
Copenhagen	코펜하겐	ko-pen-ha-gen
Dar-es-Salaam	다르에스살람	da-reu-e-seu-sal-lam
Delhi	델리	del-li
Dubai	두바이	du-ba-i

Dublin	더블린	deo-beul-lin
Düsseldorf	뒤셀도르프	dwi-sel-do-reu-peu
Florence	플로렌스	peul-lo-ren-seu
Frankfurt	프랑크푸르트	peu-rang-keu-pu-reu-teu
Geneva	제네바	je-ne-ba

Hamburg	함부르크	ham-bu-reu-keu
Hanoi	하노이	ha-no-i
Havana	아바나	a-ba-na
Helsinki	헬싱키	hel-sing-ki
Hiroshima	히로시마	hi-ro-si-ma

Hong Kong	홍콩	hong-kong
Istanbul	이스탄불	i-seu-tan-bul
Jerusalem	예루살렘	ye-ru-sal-lem
Kolkata (Calcutta)	캘커타	kael-keo-ta
Kuala Lumpur	콸라룸푸르	kwal-la-rum-pu-reu

Kyiv	키예프	ki-ye-peu
Lisbon	리스본	ri-seu-bon
London	런던	reon-deon
Los Angeles	로스앤젤레스	ro-seu-aen-jel-le-seu
Lyons	리옹	ri-ong
Madrid	마드리드	ma-deu-ri-deu

Marseille	마르세유	ma-reu-se-yu
Mexico City	멕시코시티	mek-si-ko-si-ti
Miami	마이애미	ma-i-ae-mi
Montreal	몬트리올	mon-teu-ri-ol
Moscow	모스크바	mo-seu-keu-ba

Mumbai (Bombay)	봄베이, 뭄바이	bom-be-i, mum-ba-i
Munich	뮌헨	mwin-hen
Nairobi	나이로비	na-i-ro-bi
Naples	나폴리	na-pol-li
New York	뉴욕	nyu-yok

| Nice | 니스 | ni-seu |
| Oslo | 오슬로 | o-seul-lo |

Ottawa	오타와	o-ta-wa
Paris	파리	pa-ri
Prague	프라하	peu-ra-ha
Rio de Janeiro	리우데자네이루	ri-u-de-ja-ne-i-ru
Rome	로마	ro-ma
Saint Petersburg	상트페테르부르크	sang-teu-pe-te-reu-bu-reu-keu
Seoul	서울	seo-ul
Shanghai	상하이	sang-ha-i
Singapore	싱가포르	sing-ga-po-reu
Stockholm	스톡홀름	seu-tok-ol-leum
Sydney	시드니	si-deu-ni
Taipei	타이베이	ta-i-be-i
The Hague	헤이그	he-i-geu
Tokyo	도쿄	do-kyo
Toronto	토론토	to-ron-to
Venice	베니스	be-ni-seu
Vienna	빈	bin
Warsaw	바르샤바	ba-reu-sya-ba
Washington	워싱턴	wo-sing-teon

www.ingramcontent.com/pod-product-compliance
Lightning Source LLC
Chambersburg PA
CBHW061953070426
42450CB00011BA/2816